The Articulate Advisor

Build Stronger, Lasting Relationships

Learn the process of selling through

influential communication and the power of

building trust, comfort, and confidence

with your customers!

© 2020 Lulu Author. All rights reserved.

ISBN 978-1-304-050908

FOREWORD

It is no longer a myth that articulation of value is a key factor to always bear in mind when it comes to sales. Prospects are naturally drawn to a designation of value and as a result are careful about their decisions to either buy from you or become a repeat client.

This is because the level of competition in the marketplace is excessively high and everyone is trying to get the best services to match their desired needs.

Sales simply put, is a system where money is exchanged for value. Therefore, the ability for one to recognize this pact will go a long way in separating you from the competition.

For a salesperson to render value and remain consistent at it, the mastery of effective communication cannot be overlooked.

Communicating effectively starts from brand clarity. If you want prospects to deal with you and not fall short of your promises, you must make your services clear so they can differentiate between what is required and what is not.

A true value proposition is one that paints a clear picture of what your brand has to offer to prospects.

That way, there will be communication that leads to offering smart services which in turn leads to building a reputable brand.

Apart from establishing communication, as one who offers financial services, you should avoid structuring your services to solve low value problems. This means going on to understand the pain of your prospects not just scratching the surface.

As a sales consultant, I can attest to the fact that the amount of money you make from any transaction is based on how well you understand the pain of the marketplace. Having a clear picture of the marketplace pain, will help you solve more problems from your prospects, offer value consistently, establish a credible brand and keep them happily ever after.

Being a salesperson gives you leverage on flexibility, freedom, consistent learning and unlimited earning power. It also equips you with the ability to solve problems thereby positioning you as an authority in dishing out value and crushing life principles.

Another beautiful thing about sales is that it is a performance-based career the more you sell, the more you earn. Developing the right attitude towards sales will enable you to become a better sales person.

Cut to the chase, this book unravels most of the hidden secrets to having a better understanding of the process and becoming a successful salesperson. The author "Anthony Solimini", is one who has gone through the process, seen the thrill and remains outstanding with consistency in rendering quality sales services to prospects and also empowering sales professionals from all walks of life.

Chapter 1

WHAT IS SALES?

Everything done in this world is a sale. You either sell to yourself or you sell to others.

Chapter 1

What is Sales?

As a sales person, what is "sales" to you? Is it just a means of livelihood? Is it all about meeting quotas and earning commissions or is sales something that you love doing?

If you view sales as just a job, then you will more than likely get into a situation where you start to fear quotas and sooner or later you'll get discouraged if you're not meeting them. In the end, you will likely lose your job or be forced to join another company.

Successful sales people don't consider this field as "just a job". To them, "sales" is a way of living. They are not worried about meeting quotas, for they enjoy what they are doing day in and day out.

If you do not enjoy meeting total strangers, getting to know them, and convincing them that whatever product you're offering will actually be beneficial to them, then maybe sales is not the career you're looking for.

If you're into sales only because of the potential earnings, then there might come a time when those earnings will just remain to be a potential.

The first thing you need to know and understand about "sales" is that it is something that you need to enjoy doing. Now, a lot of successful sales people never thought that they would enjoy their careers when they first started. A lot of them wanted to quit early in the game and look for a stable paying job.

However, when they learned the true secrets of sales and they started to incorporate those secrets into their selling techniques, they found out that they actually started to enjoy selling. Reaping the benefits of becoming a successful sales person only came second to them.

Every sales person needs to go out into the field day after day. To them, every day is either an opportunity to meet new customers or a day to close a sale or both.

Every sales person knows that "sales" is just a game of numbers. The more people they talk to, the higher their chances of closing a deal.

Successful sales people are motivated. There is something that will drive them to go out into the field, meet new people, face objections and rejections, every single day.

It would be good to sit down sometime and ask yourself these questions:

- As a sales person, what does "sales" mean to you?

- What is your motivation?
- What are you trying to accomplish?

What are the traits of the best sales people?

Before we go into the traits of the best sales people, let's first take a look at the traits that every sales person needs to have. These are just the basic traits of a sales person. Every sales person needs to have these traits or they would not really be considered as being one.

- Product knowledge
- Market knowledge
- Customer Centric

Product Knowledge

How can you sell your product if you don't even know what it is? If you haven't the slightest clue of what it is you are trying to sell, then how can you convince your customers to buy?

As a sales person, you need to know every single detail about your product. If you're selling a piece of wooden furniture, you need to know exactly what the type of wood was used and where it came from. You need to know the characteristics of the wood. You need to know its strengths and weaknesses.

It would be best to avoid getting into a situation where the customer knows more than you about your product. You, as the sales person, are the master of your product. There must never be a situation where you are asked a question about the product and your answer is "give me a moment to refer to our technical department". No! YOU are the sales person and you represent every single department of your company.

You might be thinking that becoming a master of your product would be too difficult for you and your job is just to sell whatever it is the company wants you to sell. If this is the way you think about your job as a sales person, then you will likely or most have likely, lost deals just because you weren't able to answer a question about your product.

Market knowledge

How well do you know your market? Is your market just a group of certain people within a certain age range or income bracket? If you really know your market, then you would also know the personalities of the people who would most likely buy your product.

If you're selling to the right market and wondering why you're not meeting your sales targets, then the most likely problem is that you really don't know your market at all.

One thing that you should remember when selling is that not everybody within a certain age range or income bracket will have exactly the same personalities. Not all of them will have the same views about the product you are selling. You will not be able to approach every single one of them exactly the same way.

Knowing your market means that you know what type of personalities you would likely face. If you have a good idea of their personalities, then you will know how to approach them and communicate with them.

As a sales person, you are a profiler. You need to be able to gauge your customer's personality within the first few minutes of talking to them. In fact, the moment you see a person, you need to be able to have a general idea of what that person's personality is.

Market knowledge is extremely important to a sales person. Without the right market knowledge, deals that should have been closed will not be. Sales opportunities are lost. In the worst case scenario, you may actually be giving the wrong impression about your product and your company.

Customer Centric

If the customer is not at the center of your universe, you are not customer centric. Therefore, you are not a true sales person.

As a sales person, the customer is your life. Everything you say and do will need to be focused on meeting the needs of your customer.

You may know every single detail about your product and you may have an in-depth knowledge about your market, but if the customer is not at the center of your universe, then you will most likely fail as a sales person.

Believe it or not, there are sales people who are very knowledgeable about their products. In fact, they are so knowledgeable that they have a need to prove the customer wrong if the customer says something that they cannot agree with.

These sales people may not get to the point where they find themselves in a heated argument with the customer (though there are sales people who do), but they have a need to prove that they were right and the customer was wrong.

Now, just because the customer is supposed to be at the center of your universe because you are customer centric, it doesn't mean that the customer is always right. However, with the right tactic, you will be able to prove the customer wrong and still get the sale.

How about the best sales people?

The best sales people are the masters of their products, they know their markets like the back of their hands and their customers are at the center of their universe. However, they have a few more traits that make them special.

Conversationalists

The best sales people know how to start and manage a conversation with their customers. Not just any conversation, but a conversation that will ultimately end up closing the deal.

Have you ever heard about the story of the sales person who ended up selling a yacht to a customer who was asking directions to the pharmacy because he needed to buy medicine for a headache?

We won't go into the details of the story, but it proves that being a conversationalist is an advantage to a sales person.

As a sales person, you need to be able to turn a very simple event to your advantage. You can do that only if you are a good conversationalist and you are customer centric.

In that story, the sales person knew exactly what the customer needed, but instead of just giving directions to the customer, the sales person was able to hold a conversation and close a deal for a product that he was actually selling.

How many people do you meet every day? When you meet someone, even someone asking for directions, do you think about closing a sale with that person?

The best sales people know what, how and when to ask questions

"All you need to do is ask". You've probably heard that phrase so many times in your life. However, do you really know what it means?

Asking questions is a skill that the best sales people have managed to develop over the years. Questions lead to answers. The right questions lead to the right answers.

When you meet someone on the streets, in a corridor or a room and you ask "how are you doing?" do you really want to hear the answer? Most people ask this question for the sake of being polite, but not really concerned about the answer.

When the best sales people ask this question, they want to hear the answer. Why? They want to hear the answer because this is the first step in closing a sale.

When you ask a person how he or she is doing, you open the doors to a conversation. Whatever that person's reply is, it is an opportunity for you to create a link with that person.

The best sales people know exactly what questions to ask and when to ask them. They want to hear the answer so that they can start and then eventually lead the conversation to their advantage.

The best sales people are the customers

While the majority of sales people know why their products would be beneficial to their customers, the best sales people know why each and every customer needs to buy their product. Remember that every customer will have their own needs or opinions about your product.

A 54" flat screen TV can mean one thing for a certain customer and a totally different thing for another customer. The flat screen TV may be a dream for some customers, while other customers may perceive it as a waste of money.

If you start a product presentation with a customer who just sees it as a waste of money, you probably won't get past a few sentences. You may not even get past your first sentence before the customer walks away.

The best sales people have a buyer's perspective. They know exactly how the customer views the product and can turn that perspective into a sale. You may be wondering how you can make a person who has no interest whatsoever about your product, actually buy it.

The secret is to understand why that person has no interest at all. You can only get to this point if you can hold a conversation with the customer. You can only hold a conversation with a customer if you gain his or her attention.

Once you understand why that particular customer is not interested in the product you are selling, you have the buyer's perspective. You can then turn this perspective to your advantage by knowing exactly why and how buyers buy.

In the next chapter, we'll take a closer look at the buyer. We will understand why buyers buy, how they buy, and what motivates them to buy. Once you understand why a customer buys, you will be well on your way to closing that deal.

Chapter 2

WHY DO CUSTOMERS BUY?

Believe that everything in this world has a purpose

Chapter 2

Why do Customers Buy?

Unless the sales person knows HOW a customer buys, they will not be effective!

As a sales person, have you ever had the experience of trying to convince a married couple to buy your product? There are situations when the husband and wife see eye to eye and have the same perspective about your product. However, usually the husband will have a totally different perspective than the wife. Who do you sell to? You sell to the decision maker of course.

What if both the husband and wife have an understanding that both of them need to be able to agree on a purchase, but they have different views? Who do you sell to now? You sell to the party that doesn't want your product.

Why?

The party who wants your product is already sold so there is no reason to keep selling. All you need to do is seal the deal. The party that needs selling is the party that doesn't want your product but has equal footing in the purchasing decision.

Again, how do you sell something to a person that doesn't want to buy? First of all, there is no such thing as a person who doesn't want to buy. Everybody wants to buy... its human nature.

But, you need to know exactly why they buy. What is it that makes a person want to buy? How do customers buy? What factors need to be fulfilled for a person to make that purchasing decision?

Need Recognition and Problem Awareness

A person may show disinterest in your product, simply because you weren't giving that person recognition.

In the husband and wife scenario, you may have been enjoying selling that 54" flat screen TV to the husband, but neglected to recognize the wife. This is what many sales people do. They enjoy selling to someone who is already sold. They hate selling to someone who doesn't want to buy so they end up losing the sale altogether.

Have you ever heard a sales person saying *"the husband wanted to buy, but I lost the sale because the wife didn't want to"*? Why were you selling to the husband? Why weren't you selling to the wife? By neglecting to pay attention to the needs of the wife, you turned her into your enemy, not knowing that they needed to make an important decision together.

Sometimes, all a person really needs to buy is some recognition and problem awareness. As a sales person, you need to be aware of the things that make a person not want to buy. What is their concern?

The wife may be the one in the family who balances their checking account and concerned that the purchase make bring them under. You were selling to the husband who just wanted the TV.

If you recognized the wife and found out exactly what the problem was, you may have been able to get her on your side by empathizing with her situation.

Information Search

There are times when a customer buys because the need for information has been fulfilled. In the husband and wife scenario, you were eager to discuss the technical details of the TV set with the husband who understands a thing or two about TV's. Unfortunately, the wife doesn't understand a thing about the technical jargon that you were talking about with the husband, but she wanted to buy the TV if only she understood it.

Whenever, you make a sales presentation, make sure that everybody understands exactly what you are saying. You don't excitingly talk about how may pixels the screen has, when the person doesn't even know what a pixel is.

When you are presenting to a group and you're not sure if everybody in that group will understand the technical jargon, make sure that you explain what it is you're saying. You never know if that person who doesn't understand is actually the decision maker.

Evaluation of Alternatives

Some people want to compare products so that they are sure they will buy the best one. Their deepest concern is ending up being told by someone that they should have bought this or that product instead because it was better or cheaper.

As a sales person, you need to know what the other alternatives are to your product. You need to be able to explain the alternatives, without actually bad-mouthing other brands or companies.

Never answer a customer's concern by bad-mouthing the alternative to your product. When a customer tells you, "*oh, but the store next door is selling the exact same TV at a much lesser price*" and you say "well, you know, I've actually seen their warehouse and their stockmen are just throwing things around. They might be selling at a lower price because they know that something is wrong with their inventory."

Instead of gaining credibility, did you know that you are actually losing credibility by bad-mouthing others?

As a sales person, you need to know exactly what the alternatives are to your product and you need to be able to explain them in a way that will benefit your product without placing the other products in a bad light.

There will be some customers who just want to evaluate the alternatives and it really doesn't matter to them if whether or not the product you're selling has a higher price tag or not. They just want to understand what the alternatives are and holding an informational conversation with them is just what they need to make a purchasing decision.

Post Purchase Evaluation

There are also customers who need to know exactly what will happen once they make the purchase. Does your company provide support for the product you are selling? How fast will your company be able to provide support?

Sometimes customers just need reassurance that you won't just be taking their money and running away. As a sales person, you need to reassure your customers that they are not just important until you get their money, but they will continue to be important as long as they need you.

All of the Above

Don't be surprised if you meet customers who have all of the concerns listed above. As a sales person, you will need to handle all of their concerns so that they make the purchase.

This is precisely the reason why you need to be a good conversationalist. Every customer is a sale waiting to happen. Find out exactly what the concerns of your customer are, and if it just so happens that all of the above are their concerns, then be patient and handle them one by one.

Now, how exactly do you find out what their concerns are?

The only way you're going to find the answer to this question is if you have a process. Every sales person needs to have a process and that process needs to be in-line with the buying process of the customer. Every customer has a buying process that they follow and if your sales process does not agree with their buying process, you will lose that sale.

In the next chapter, we will take a closer look at the sales process and see exactly how this process can be tuned to the customer buying process.

Chapter 3

The S.A.L.E.S = $OLD Process

The only thing you can achieve without a process is

NOTHING

Chapter 3

The Sales Process

S.A.L.E.S = $OLD

In the previous chapter we took a look at the factors that influence the buyer's decision. We answered the question *"Why do buyers buy?"*, and we discovered that every customer has a customer process that needs to be fulfilled before the purchase is made.

The best way to fulfill a customer's process is to have a sales process that will provide an answer to all of the concerns of the customer. This process is called S.A.L.E.S

> **S = Set the scene**
>
> **A = Adapt to the audience**
>
> **L = Listen and Learn**
>
> **E = Evaluate and Explain**
>
> **S = Sign and Seal the Deal!**

Handling objections is one of the most critical steps in any sales process. If a customer's concerns or objections are not solved right then and there, the likelihood of losing the sale becomes very high.

Always remember that the longer it takes to handle an objection, the more the customer will lose interest in purchasing your product.

No matter how large or how small or how totally out-of-this-world the objection may be, it is your job as a sales person to see to it that the objection is met with a viable solution. Of course, you won't be able to provide solutions to all the customer's concerns and you won't be able to win every sale because there is no such thing as a 100% batting average in sales, but you will be able to decrease the number of lost sales due to poor salesmanship if you learn how to handle objections.

This is precisely the reason why you need a sales process. A sales process enables you to lead the customer into a situation where you have the upper hand. If you carry out your sales process carefully, there is a very good chance that you will need to handle fewer objections and close the sale early.

Every sales person should already have a sales process that they can implement. If you already have one, you should be able to tie-in the following sales process with yours. If not, then study this sales process and implement it.

Chapter 4

S = Set the Scene

Create the stage and you can control the play

Chapter 4

S = Set the Scene

As a sales person, are you always aware of the situation you are getting into? If not, then this is the first thing that you should be working on. Setting the scene means knowing the battle field ahead of time.

Before you even start your product presentation, you should already be aware of the following information:

Who are the decision makers? Who within the organization will most likely influence the decision makers? Who are the audience of your product presentation? Are they the decision makers or those who will influence the decision?

In some cases, especially if you're selling to a large organization, you may not be able to present to the decision makers off the bat. Don't worry as you will most likely be presenting to the people within the organization that will more than likely influence the decision makers.

If this is the case, even though they aren't the decision makers, you will still need to do your best. There are some sales people who think that just because they aren't talking to the decision makers, they don't need to do a full product presentation. This is risky because your company may have competitors in your industry and if your competitors impress the customer with their presentation then they will likely be the ones to present to the decision makers.

Think of this as different levels of a job interview. Before you get to be interviewed by the President or General Manager of the company, or whoever is going to sign your employment papers, you will most likely go through interviews with the people who will recommend you for employment.

Remember that in the previous chapter we talked about a customer's need to be recognized. If you do not recognize all the important people in the organization, you may end up losing the sale because you failed to recognize someone who could directly influence the purchasing decision.

What is your strategy? If you're working a key account, your strategy must already have been tried, tested and proven to work with large clients. Whatever your strategy is, never lose your focus. Setting the scene means careful preparation so you should already have a strategy in mind.

Be specific, don't generalize

"Setting the scene" means knowing precisely why your customer would be compelled to buy your product. Of course you already know the strengths and weaknesses of your product you wouldn't be a salesperson if you didn't. However, do you know exactly why the customer you will be presenting to would be compelled to buy it?

If you already know why this particular customer needs your product, you can focus your sales presentation on this reason instead of generalizing your presentation. When you customize your sales presentation to meet a certain customer's needs, the chances are higher that your presentation will be appreciated thus you will likely close the deal.

Now, if you're going to sell to a large organization, you'll have enough time to find out about the company and how your product would benefit them the most. However, if you're in a showroom and a potential customer walks up to you, you won't have that much time to figure this out. What you can do is ask questions. Get the customer involved in a conversation and make sure that the customer understands that you are there not just to sell, but to provide a solution to the needs of the customer.

When you ask questions, make sure that you are listening. You may be thinking that it would only be natural for a sales person to listen when he or she asks a question, but you'll be surprised at how many sales people don't actually "listen" to the answer when they ask questions.

Always remember that whenever a customer answers your question, the customer is giving you the opportunity to close the deal. If you weren't listening to the answer, you would already have lost that opportunity.

Whenever you ask questions to find out what the customer's compelling reason to act is, you are closing the deal. When a customer tells you why your product is needed, when it is needed and what it is needed for, then the deal is done. All you need to do is reassure the customer that their needs can and will be met, or if not, provide a viable alternative that the customer should be able to agree to.

You may be thinking, "Well… customers won't always readily give that information away". Of course not, you may need to skillfully pry that information out of them. Unless you have the charisma of a church leader, you've got your work cut out for you.

Gaining the trust and confidence of a total stranger will not be easy. It takes a long time for trust to build-up between two or more people and you have only a few minutes or days depending on the account you are working on.

Rest assured that it's going to be difficult to gain the trust of the customer, especially nowadays when most customers can already see through sales people. Customers who are very experienced in dealing with sales people know the tactics that they employ.

Most customers think that sales people will do everything to gain their business. Sales people have been known to be able to promise the world, but seemingly have various problems in delivery. They are also known to be very friendly when asking for the customer's money, but turn into a snob when delivery or product problems creep up in the future.

Keep in mind that customers will most likely buy from people who they perceive are their friends or have gained their trust. Your primary objective as a sales person is to gain your customer's trust. This is exactly why you need to be an excellent conversationalist if you want to be included in the ranks of the best salesmen.

How exactly will you be able to gain your customer's trust in a matter of a few minutes?

The best sales people have different methods that they use to gain a customer's trust. It is important to remember that there is no one method that will work for every customer.

Every customer has his or her own personality, traits and beliefs. If you have two sales people from the same company selling the same product side by side in front of a customer, it will only be natural for the customer to like one but not the other.

The question is how will you be able to increase the chances of being the sales person that the customer likes and trusts?

Trust is a two-way street. You can't trust someone without knowing that the other person trusts you as well. You can't like someone without getting the feeling that the other person likes you as well.

As sales professionals, we are expected to "like" everybody. Every single person we meet on the streets is a potential customer. Everybody is a sale waiting to happen.

Okay, so you may be dealing with a highly specialized product that not everybody will be able to buy. You may be selling a multi-million dollar house and not everybody you'll meet on the streets will have the resources to become your customer.

This is definitely true, but do you know everybody you meet on the street? You may be sitting beside a wealthy decision maker on the bus or train to work and not even know it. The person on the other table in a restaurant may be an influencer to a decision maker.

As a sales person, if you do not like everybody, then you are severely limiting your market.

A man walks into a car showroom poorly dressed and even forgot to shave that morning. The showroom happened to be dealing cars that were way above the average person's paycheck. Now, the man who walked in looked pretty much average.

Let's say that you worked as a sales person inside that showroom. You expect to be meeting wealthy customers so you are well dressed every single day. You know that you need to be very presentable for your customers to trust you.

The question is, would you judge that person who walked in according to his appearance and refuse to entertain him? Would you do your job as a sales person and entertain that person like every other customer who walks in?

It is true that we need to know our market. As such, you will already have projected a mental image of a possible customer. You have made the decision on what type of person you can like.

Would you still be able to think that what if that gentleman who walked in was in fact a very hard working business executive who closed the deal of the decade late last night and wasn't able to go home yet. What if he was in your showroom to look for a car to buy for his wife as a present?

Now, this business executive was an excellent, maybe the best, sales person because he was able to close the deal of the decade. If you did not entertain him the same way you would with your other customers, you will have lost a sale.

As a sales person, you do not have the luxury of picking the people you want to like. It is your job to like everybody. You can't stand on a street corner, watching the people go buy choosing which ones will have the resources to buy your product.

It really doesn't matter what it is you are selling. Remember that story about the sales person who was able to sell a yacht to someone looking for medicine for a headache? That sales person was selling a product worth thousands of dollars but still had time to entertain someone who really wasn't even looking to buy a yacht.

It is not your product that defines you. YOU define your product.

Just because you're selling a million dollars worth of property does not mean that you need to think that you can only entertain those who "look" as if they were capable of buying your product. Keep in mind that every customer is a sale waiting to happen.

If you cannot or you are not even willing to gain the trust of everybody you meet, then your market has just been limited to the mental image of an "ideal" customer that you created in your mind.

In order to gain a customer's trust, you first need to trust your customer. You can only do this if you learn how to display trust everybody. Do not get into the habit of choosing the customers you want to trust.

This is the common mistake of sales people. They think that their time is severely limited as such they need to use their time wisely. They will only entertain those who they think are capable of buying their product. Do not make this mistake.

Showing genuine trust to a customer is a part of creating rapport. This is a skill that every sales person needs to develop. In the following chapter we will discuss the skill of creating rapport. We will go into the details of creating rapport and how it is used to increase our sales.

Chapter 5

A = Adapt to the Audience

Reach for the Hearts of Your Audience

Chapter 5

A = Adapt to the Audience

"*Birds of the same feather flock together*". It is only human nature for a person to get along better with someone or a group of people with similar characteristics. People tend to trust those they can get along with. As a sales person, you'll need to be a chameleon. You need to be any type of bird so that you can go with any type of flock. You need to trust and be trusted by any type of person.

You, as a person, will have your own traits, your own characteristics, your own personality, and you will most likely go out with groups that have similar personalities, traits and characteristics. However, as a salesperson you will need to be very flexible and be able to adapt to your audience. This means, whatever the personality, traits, and characteristics the person you are selling to has, you will need to display them as well.

Creating Rapport

The first thing you should do when you are in front of a customer is to create rapport. Have you ever had the experience of someone you just met saying "I feel as if I've known you for ages"? What exactly happened was that you were able to create rapport, and as a sales person, everybody you meet should be feeling this way.

To create rapport is to create a bond between you and the other person or group of people. The other person must feel that you understand them. They must feel that you are a person they can trust. If you are able to create rapport, the other person will be confident that whatever you are offering will actually be beneficial to them because they trust you.

Some people have the ability to create rapport almost instantly. They can go up to anybody, say hi or hello, and the next thing you know, they're talking to that person as if they were the best of friends. It's as if they have this kind of charisma with other people.

Could it be the way they speak or the way they dress? Is it their outward appearance that helps them to become instantly likeable? Is the ability to create rapport something that people are born with, or is it something that can be developed? Has it something to do with your personality?

Creating rapport is yes to all those questions. It is the way a person speaks and dresses. It is also partly because of the outward appearance. It is something that everybody is born with and it can be developed. It has everything to do with your personality.

As a sales person, it is absolutely critical that you have the ability to create rapport with everybody.

Rapport is a skill that you cannot do without. Without this skill, your growth as a sales person will be stunted and your career will not go very far.

Creating rapport does not mean you need to be a movie actor or actress. Creating rapport is not a script of a role you need to play. Creating rapport is you as a person.

Creating rapport is actually the process of befriending the other person to gain that person's trust. If what you do does not come naturally, you will likely fail in your objective as people will be able to see right through you.

Creating rapport is about sincerity. You should always be asking yourself if you are trying to gain that person's trust only because you want their business, or are you sincere in your objective to befriend them.

In order to become the best in your field, you need to be sincere with your customers. How can you provide a solution to their needs if you're only interested in selling your product? How will you even know exactly what they need if the only thoughts that run in your mind is closing the deal?

Sincerity is one of the biggest problems of many sales people. "Sales" is a game of numbers. The more people you talk to, the more sales you are likely to achieve. This is why you will often see many sales people jump from one customer to another in order to increase the amount of people they meet.

Unfortunately, many sales people have forgotten how to be sincere. They can only show a certain amount of sincerity if the customer they are talking to shows a certain amount of interest in their product. If a customer is not interested, the sales person is not interested as well. To the sales person, time is of the essence and they simply do not have the time to be sincere to everybody.

Every customer is a sale waiting to happen. That sale may not be now, tomorrow, a week or even year from now, but it is a sale waiting to happen. The only thing that will prevent it from happening is a lack of sincerity on your part as a sales person.

When you create rapport you create friends. You create a group of people who trust you. All of your customers will belong to a group of people who trusts them too. If that customer does not buy from you for any reason, there is still a possibility that you can be recommended to the customer's group.

When you create rapport with a customer, you open a door to a lot of sales opportunities. This is exactly why we say that every customer is a sale waiting to happen. That sale may not be with that customer particularly, it can possibly be with a friend of that customer.

As a sales person, the more doors you open the more sales you get and it all starts with creating rapport with a single customer.

How many customers do you meet every day? Have you been able to create rapport with every single one of them?

You may be thinking that some customers will not even give you the chance to create rapport. You may be cold calling, house to house or office to office and you find that customers simply slam the door in your face. How then would you be able to create rapport?

First of all, cold calling is one of the least effective selling strategies. It is a waste of time and resources. This isn't to say that you won't be able to get a sale. You could possibly get a sale from cold calling, but the chances are so slim that it really isn't worth your time.

If you have the ability to create rapport, there shouldn't be a need for cold calling. Every customer you were able to close a sale with should have become your friend.

Okay, so you're thinking "that's good in theory but it isn't possible in the real world." Why? How many friends have you got? Do you belong to a tight group of friends and all of your customers were just acquaintances?

Now, think about how sincere you were with all of your past customers. If they ended up just being a customer, then do you really think you were successful at creating rapport?

Creating rapport is not about closing the deal. Closing the deal is a possible and likely end result of creating rapport, but it is not the primary objective.

The primary objective of creating rapport is to create a bond between you and your customer. That bond may enable you to close that deal, but it should also enable you to find many more deals to close. This is the reason why you shouldn't be cold calling in the first place.

You simply do not have the time to be cold calling. Your time should be spent with your friends. You should be trying to become friends with their friends.

Creating rapport is the life and soul of every sales person. If you do not know how to create rapport, you're just a banner ad, you are a billboard, and you are definitely not a sales person.

How exactly do you create rapport?

Have you ever been in a conversation with someone who just nods their head or gives you a blank stare while you're talking? You will surely get the feeling that the other person has no interest in you whatsoever.

Did you ever wonder why that other person was not interested? Maybe you didn't even spend the time to think about it and just moved on to another customer.

If a person gives you a blank stare or doesn't have any interest in you or what you are saying, it is obvious that you failed to create rapport.

Remember that your primary objective to creating rapport is not to close a deal. You are creating rapport to create a bond; to create friendship.

Many sales people think that creating rapport is all about selling. Even sales seminars will often tell you to create rapport. Sales people are often taught to create rapport. Rapport is a big word in sales, but unfortunately, many people get it wrong.

The difference between an average sales person and an excellent sales person is their understanding of what creating rapport really means. The best sales people do not even need to look for their sales because sales just seem to come to them. This is because they understand what creating rapport really means.

The first step to creating rapport is becoming sincere in your objective to make your customer your friend. You need to be sincere in creating that bond or you will not be able to create rapport. You may be able to get that sale, but you may also have failed in your objective to make your customer your friend.

If you want to create rapport, you need to show genuine interest in the person or people you are talking to. You need to listen to what they are saying and react accordingly. You need to be able to speak to them as a friend and the only way to accomplish this is to show your sincerity.

Now, you must have a friend or two. How do you speak to your friends? Are you genuinely concerned about what is happening in their lives? If they have a problem, do you really want to help? Can you feel their joy or their grief? Are you willing to go out of your way to help a friend in need?

In order to create rapport, you need to see your customer as one of your friends; someone who you can talk to like a friend; someone who you are genuinely interested in; and someone who you would go out of your way to help.

The way you think about someone will show in your behavior. If you are intimidated with someone, you will display a certain amount of nervousness. If you don't care about someone, you will naturally show a certain amount of disinterest.

People know what you truly feel because they have friends too. They know how their friends communicate with them. Now, if you communicate the same way as their friends communicate with them, they will naturally feel at ease with you and rapport can be created.

The key to creating rapport is to show genuine interest in the person you are talking to. Remember that communication does not necessarily need to be verbal. Your actions or even your eyes can communicate.

You need to feel at ease with the person you are talking to. If you do not feel at ease with your customer, how do you expect your customer to feel at ease with you?

It is easy to show interest in another person if you feel at ease with them. Now, remember that you need to make it look natural or the other person will think that you are faking it. The secret is to think that you are talking to a friend. Think of your customer as your friend and you will definitely act as if you were talking to a friend.

You can show your interest by showing your curiosity about them. They need to feel that you want to know more about them, their life, their beliefs, practically everything there is to know. Now, of course you won't be going into a conversation about every detail of their life. Your customer just needs to feel that you would be interested if that conversation ever did come up.

Remember that you are trying to create a friend so in the future you can expect to actually have a conversation like this with your customer, hopefully your new found friend.

You create rapport when you see the world the way they see it. You don't necessarily have to agree, but you will need to be willing to understand their views and opinions. In a sales conversation, you do not want to let the conversation get out of hand to where you can't control it. If you let the conversation get into a topic about views and opinions, you may find it difficult to bring it back to your objective.

It's true that you want to create a friend, but you can leave the discussion about views and opinions for a later date. For now, your objective is to create a friend so that you can discuss your product. You are a business person and you are holding a business conversation, so keep it that way.

If there are sales people who have a problem with creating rapport, there are also sales people who have a problem with keeping rapport under control. They find that they can easily make friends, but they have difficulty in controlling the conversation.

Your primary objective in creating rapport is to create a bond, but don't forget your objective of selling as well. You will have plenty of time to create a much stronger bond when you do after sales supports and follow-ups.

Neuro-linguistic Programming

Have you ever heard of the term "neuro-linguistic programming"? It seems to be all technical and stuff, but what it is really, is to gain a better understanding of a person by adapting to their verbal and non-verbal responses.

Everybody has a certain method of talking. Some talk fast as if they were just thinking out loud. Others talk slowly to make sure that they are understood.

Have you ever noticed how newscasters talk? Did you notice that they talk clearly and at a pitch that is neither too high nor too low? They seem to talk without any emotion even if the news they are reporting can be a bit emotional.

Now, newscasters don't necessarily talk that way behind the camera. They have their own natural way of talking. They only talk that way in front of the camera because they are required to.

As a sales person you won't have to talk like a newscaster, but you will need to adapt to another person's way of talking if you want to create rapport. You need to adapt to the way that person speaks, the language that person uses, and his or her gestures.

People who talk in a certain manner will most likely find it easier to understand those who talk in the same way.

In order to create rapport, you need to "understand" the person you are talking to and that person needs to understand you as well. Once you understand that person, you are in the position to gain that person's trust and confidence.

A technique that is widely used to create rapport is match and mirror. In match and mirror, you attempt to be as similar as possible to the person you are talking to, without actually copying them. If you copy, they will most likely feel that you are insulting them.

Match and mirror does not mean to copy but to come close so that you reach a point where you are understood. It can be difficult to do and at times a bit risky because if you over do it you run the risk of imitating and that is not good.

You can match and mirror the following:

Physiology – You can try to match and mirror a person's posture, breathing and gestures. However, if the other person has some disabilities, be careful not to match and mirror those as well. For example: if a person limps while walking or has spontaneous limb spasms, be careful not to mirror them.

Voice – Try to match voice quality, tempo, timbre, and volume as close as possible. If the other person is very high or low pitched, go as high or low as you can without over acting. You should still be able to speak as if it were natural to you.

Language - Pay close attention to how the other person speaks. You will need to be able to use the same language they do. If they use any jargon, use the same jargon. People want to be able to talk with other people of the same level as them.

As a sales person, you will need to quickly understand your customer, including his or her personality. A way to do this is to become familiar with DISC profiling.

DISC Profiling

In DISC profiling, the personalities of people are grouped into four quadrants:

    D = Dominance

    I = Influence

    S = Steadiness

    C = Compliance

D= Dominance

People who are in this group are all about control. They are very assertive and have a natural love for power. These are people who talk about themselves, their goals and their values. They want change and they want results.

Dominant people want to feel that they are in control. However, they also like other people who are confident and assertive. When talking to people in this group, you need to be very confident about yourself and you need to be assertive. However, do not overdo it. Remember that you should match and mirror, but not to the point that the other person gets the impression that you feel you are above them.

Dominant people talk in a very assertive way. Every word that they say will seem to have been said with a purpose. They ask questions and they want to hear the answer because they want that answer to convince them.

As a salesperson, you also need to show a bit of a dominant personality. You need to be able to speak with conviction. You need to know your product and you need to know it like the back of your hand or you will not seem convincing.

When a dominant person asks you a question, make sure that you answer that question precisely and then you attempt for an explanation, not the other way around.

When you are presenting a product to a group of decision makers, you will most likely be faced with a group of dominant people. As you try to analyze them, know that they are trying to analyze you as well. They want to analyze you because they want to know if you are telling the truth. They want to know if they can trust you and everything you say and do, even your gestures, and how you move your eyes will have a meaning to them.

Dominant decision makers are leaders and they will respect those who have the ability to lead as well. One of the reasons why sales presentations for major clients or customers are done by senior sales personnel is because they also show leadership qualities.

This is important because the only way you can convince a dominant person is if you talk and move the same way. You will find it difficult if not impossible to convince a dominant person if you act as if you cannot even convince yourself. If you are talking to a dominant person, speak with conviction or you will not be able to create rapport.

I = Influence

People who fall under this group tend to be emotional, but they are very social. They love to influence others as such they have quite a magnetic personality. They normally talk about themselves, the future, good things, team-spirit, and other people.

You need to be a bit careful when talking to people under this group as they can easily "lead" a conversation. As a sales person, you need to be able to control a conversation and lead it to where it would be beneficial for your sale.

You can easily warm-up to people under this group and if you perform correctly, they will also easily warm-up to you.

As a salesperson, you need to belong to this category. You need to have the ability to influence other people.

S = Steadiness

The people who fall under this group are those who like to go on a steady pace. They do not like sudden changes as they want to feel security. They are normally calm, consistent, and deliberate. They are very unemotional so it would be difficult to identify what they are feeling.

These are the people who talk about agreements and principles. They like to associate the past with the present situations. It isn't difficult to deal with the people under this group as all they really need to feel is that you are consistent with what you are saying. You will have to give them a sense of security in your personality.

C = Compliance

Those who fall under this category love to follow rules and regulations. They are systematic in what they do, so make sure that whatever you present them is in order. They want to deal with facts so present the facts as clearly as you can and in a systematic way that they will appreciate.

Do not mistake these people as being pushovers. They may like to follow rules and regulations, but this does not mean that they lack self will. They follow rules and regulations because they believe in a system.

A system means that everything is organized. They believe that whatever rule or regulation they are following has a purpose.

How will you know when rapport has been established?

You will know when you have successfully established rapport when the other person starts talking to you as an equal or as a friend. You will start to have a better conversation as they will start to open-up and let their guard down. You will also know when they start seeking your advice or your opinion about something. When you get the feeling that the other person is comfortable around you, then you have established rapport.

Once you have established rapport, be careful not to suddenly change your personality. Remember that you have your own personality and this could easily show once you get comfortable yourself. Always remain focused on your objective and that is to close the deal.

It's true that you want to create rapport or a bond between you and your customer so that you can open up doors for future sales. It would be difficult to act like a person you're not if you happen to be able to create a friendship.

DISC profiling and match & mirroring are not about creating a false you. It is about understanding the person you are talking to so that you can create a bond. This is why you do not want to imitate.

Think about your own group of friends. Do you act the way they do? Do you speak the way they do? Probably not, but you are still friends with them. You understand your friends and they understand you. You and your friends have something in common and that is what rapport is all about.

This is exactly what DISC profiling is all about. You need to understand your customer so you can find a common point of interest. By understanding your customer's personality, you'll have a bigger chance of creating rapport.

However, it is important to understand that DISC profiling is only a single tool in establishing rapport. In the end, it will be your personality that the customer will like or dislike. As a sales professional, you will be responsible for developing your own personality. You will need to become someone who the majority of customers will find it easy to get along with.

Chapter 6

L = Listen & Learn

Listen and you will understand

Understand and you will Learn

Chapter 6

L = Listen and Learn

An integral part of understanding is listening. If you don't listen, you won't understand. No matter what group a person may fall in the DISC quadrant, you have to carefully listen. Listening is your key to establishing rapport.

In any conversation, never act like you're dumb. If you do not understand, let the other person know and have it explained a little further. This way you will learn. People love it when they are able to pass something on to another person.

Never pretend that you know what a person is talking about when you really don't. Believe it or not, it is easy to spot people who pretend that they know something. It will be much better to ask questions about a certain topic that came up in the conversation.

However, keep in mind that you need to take control of the conversation. Whenever you find that the conversation is falling away from you, lead it back to where you want it to go. You should already have a mental list of questions that you need to ask so that you understand what the person needs, when it is needed, and what it is needed for.

Listen carefully to what your customer is saying, because the information that you are looking for may have already come out, just not the way you were expecting it to. Watch carefully for non-verbal reactions.

For example, if you were selling a house to a couple and the wife or the husband starts talking about how their friends, children or other family members would love this and that part of the house, you would already know that this is the house they are looking for. At this point, you can already attempt to close the deal.

If you develop your listening skills, you can easily identify buying signals. Once you have the buying signals, attempt a close. If the customer has more concerns, address these concerns, listen for buying signals and attempt another close.

Not all of your customers will be easy to get along with. Some may have beliefs that are totally different from yours. Unfortunately, in the "Listen & Learn" part, you need to understand them. In understanding, your own beliefs may become a hindrance.

Do not let your feelings, emotions or beliefs interfere with your listening and understanding ability. Remember that it is not necessary for you to agree with your customer's beliefs. As long as you understand what your customer is saying, it is enough for your customer to feel at ease with you.

Again, when you're listening and trying to understand, keep focused on your objectives. There will be times when you will need to help the customer by asking questions that have answers that will lead you back to your objectives. Never let the conversation get out of hand as you may find that the customer suddenly loses track of time and remembers some other important thing to do.

Listen and learn whatever it is the customer wants to discuss, but lead the conversation back to your product. This way, you can actually help the customer make a buying decision.

Socratic Method of Discussion

When a conversation starts moving away from your topic, there will always be a trigger or a starting point.

For example: Let's say that you are selling a car and having a great conversation with your customer. Your conversation goes into the speed of the car and the brake system. The customer eagerly talks about speed and brakes and goes into some theory about momentum and examples of how a relative or a friend got into an accident.

You notice that the customer is moving away from the main topic and that is to buy the car. You want to lead the conversation back, but it would be rather impolite to cut the customer off. The best thing to do is to look for opportunities to ask questions that would lead the conversation back to the speed and braking capability of the car you are selling.

A good question would be like *"this car has such and such a brake system installed, would you happen to know if the car your friend was in had the same system?"*

The answer would be a yes, no, or doesn't know, but from here you can talk about how the safety features of the car would benefit the customer.

If you were listening attentively, you would also have figured out that the customer was in fact relaying to you a concern. By mentioning an accident because of a brake failure or something related to your original discussion, the customer is concerned about safety and may be looking for reassurance.

The above scenario is actually an example of the Socratic Method of Discussion. In this method, you ask questions that will lead to a conclusion that you desire.

Your question was if the customer knew if the other car had the same brake system installed. The customers answer was a yes, no, or didn't know. No matter what the customer's answer was, your reply would be of course to promote the safety aspect of the vehicle you were selling and the conclusion would be that your vehicle was safe or even safer.

Not only would you have lead the conversation back to your desired objective, but you also helped the customer understand more about your vehicle and come to a conclusion.

Leading the conversation is a skill that master sales people have been able to develop over years of talking to customers. They were only able to develop this skill be learning how to listen and learn effectively.

By listening attentively, the best sales people know exactly what type of questions to ask. They know the situations wherein they should ask open or closed ended questions. In leading a conversation, it is important for you to know exactly what type of question to ask in what situation.

Open-ended questions

What are open ended questions and when should you be asking them?

Open-ended questions should only be asked if you want to solicit more information about a particular subject. Try not to make your open ended question too generalized.

For example: "How do you do?" or "How are you doing today?" are opened ended questions normally used as an ice breaker. These questions are way too general and to some people they really don't have any meaning anymore. These questions are used too often that people don't really think that they require an answer.

A customer who might be feeling exceptionally conversational that day may end up giving you answer of how great he or she was feeling because of something that happened. On the other hand, the customer may not be feeling too good but was willing to tell you about why he or she was having a lousy day.

The customer may also not want to be conversational and will just politely tell answer "I'm fine, thank you".

Now, as a sales person you know that you need to lead the conversation so you're eager to get down to business. However, you will need to show a bit of empathy first before you start with your presentation.

Many sales people would answer with a "Great! I'm glad that you're having a great day…" or "I'm sorry to hear that, but I think I may just have something to make your day better…" or the sales person would dive in a bit more to find out exactly what caused the customer's feeling.

There is nothing wrong with using this type of open-ended question as an ice breaker, but be careful that you show sincerity in your answer. Customers are used to sales people asking them how they were doing. Imagine a customer who has already seen several different sales people before you and every time the sales person asked the same question. By the time you ask the question, the customer would have already been tired of hearing it over and over again.

Closed-ended questions

Open-ended questions are good ice breakers but so are closed-ended questions if used in the right way. A good way to start a closed-ended question with a customer is to ask if the customer knew about something that was most interesting about your product.

You may start with introducing yourself and go straight to asking the customer if he or she knew this and that about your product. Go straight to your product's selling points, but don't forget about creating rapport.

The advantage of mentioning the best selling point of your product early in the conversation is that you can set the scene. The customer is expecting to find out more about your product and your approach will assure the customer that you are ready to offer whatever information is needed.

The closed-ended question will usually be answered with a "no", if it pertains to something interesting about your product, unless of course the customer was already well versed about the product. In such a case, the customer may agree with you, offer an opinion and you are on with the discussion.

If you ask the right mixture of open and closed ended questions, you will be able to control the conversation. You'll be able to make your customer see your point of view by guiding the customer's logical reasoning process. When you guide the customer this way, you are actually making the customer come to a conclusion that is in your favor.

Lead but don't dominate

There is nothing more boring than listening to a sales person talk and talk and talk and talk. Never dominate a conversation. It really won't be a conversation if you're the only one talking. This is precisely the reason why you need to ask open or closed ended questions.

You need to get the customer involved in a conversation for the following reasons:

- To create rapport
- To gauge the customer's personality
- To find out the customer's concerns
- To close the deal

You won't be able to create rapport if you're the only one doing all the talking. You will not be able to tell which quadrant the customer's personality falls into. Worst of all, you will not be able to find out the concerns so you can provide a solution and close the deal.

When you do all the talking you are not matching your sales process with the customer's buying process.

Now, when you're doing a product presentation in front of the board of directors of a company, the situation may be a bit different. The presentation will normally come first before the question and answer portion.

However, the basic idea remains the same. You need to be able to capture the attention of the audience so that you can adapt.

The first few words that you speak in this situation are critical.

Let's go back in time to your college days. You've probably had quite a number of professors. Some were able to make you focus on the lecture from the beginning all the way to the end. Some on the other hand, made it very hard for you to keep your eyes open or to keep your mind from thinking about that beautiful blond or red head a couple of seats away, or maybe that varsity football player.

College professors have different styles of teaching, but can you remember what style made you really become attentive?

The teaching methods that would most have likely made you attentive were the ones that had a mixture of audience participation and a bit of humor. In short, the professor was able to create rapport and thus was able to adapt to the audience so that they would listen.

When doing a sales presentation, you must be able to apply the same techniques. Think of yourself as a professor with the need to transfer information to the audience. If you just keep talking and talking without creating an opportunity for your audience to participate, you could lose the interest of more than half of your audience in no time.

Always remember that you are presenting a product that your audience needs. Your product has value and you should present it as such. How can you convince the audience of the value of your product if they do not participate?

When you hold a discussion with a professor, you will most likely be asked questions that will ultimately lead you to make a conclusion that whatever the professor is explaining is correct and has value. The professor will make you think logically to come up with a conclusion that the professor wants you to.

The only way your audience will understand the value of your product is if they ask questions and this is exactly what you want your audience to do.

Lead the conversation but do not dominate it or else you run the risk of your audience coming up with the wrong conclusion.

Active Listening

Now, when your audience starts to participate and ask questions or offer their opinions, listen. When they start to share their concerns, listen.

Active listening is a process to ensure that you completely understood what you were listening to. When you practice active listening you either ask to confirm what you heard, or you paraphrase what you heard to confirm your understanding.

What is the importance of active listening in sales?

In sales, active listening works both ways. Your audience needs to actively listen to you so that they understand completely what you are offering and you also need to actively listen to your audience so that you understand their concerns.

If you know how to actively listen, you can also tell if your audience is actively listening to you. As a sales person you want to ensure that your audience is actively listening. Why?

First of all, there have been studies that proved that most people understand less than 50% of what they heard. In fact, the range is only about 10%. If your audience is not actively listening to you, then you know that more than half of what you tried to explain went into one ear and out the other.

If your audience is not actively listening to what you are trying to explain, your chances of closing the deal are very slim.

If there is no active listening by both parties in a conversation, it cannot be considered a conversation at all. If there is no conversation, there is no sale.

As a sales person, you need to ensure that you are actively listening to your audience when they voice their concerns or their opinions, and you also need to ensure that your audience is actively listening to you.

How exactly do you accomplish this? The answer is simple: you apply everything in this chapter into your conversation with your audience.

We covered the Socratic method of discussion, the importance of open and closed questions, and why we should lead conversations but not dominate them. All of these topics go towards creating a conversation with active listening.

When you allow audience participation, you create a conversation. When you ask open and closed questions, you force your audience to listen to you.

You also force your audience to participate more in the conversation. When you lead but not dominate the conversation, your audience will likely come up with a conclusion that you desire.

Now, here's an exercise you can do to develop your listening and learning skills and also to learn how to apply these skills in a normal manner.

It is critical that you are able to apply these skills in a normal fashion or your audience will think that you are playing with their minds. Leading your audience to come to a conclusion that you desire without them being able to actually notice what you are doing takes a lot of practice.

One way to practice is to hold a conversation with someone close to you. That person can be your wife, your husband, your children, your parents, or even a close friend. It is important that you practice on someone close to you because they can tell if you're not acting normally.

It is also important that you do not tell that person that you are in fact practicing. If you let that person know, then you really won't be able to get a genuine feedback. Now, the feedback you are looking for is not that other person telling you that you did fine. The feedback you want is for the other person to come to a conclusion that you desire.

Think about some situation that you want to happen, but the other person is sort of on the negative side. Now, your objective is of course for the other person to come to a conclusion that you want, but since you're practicing with someone close to you, this really isn't that necessary.

What is important is that you understand what the other person is saying and that you are completely understood as well. Do not let your conversation turn into an argument. You don't want to get into an argument with your customer, much more so with someone close to you.

That more natural you can get in applying what you have learned in this chapter with someone close to you, the more natural you will seem in front of a customer.

Chapter 7

E = Evaluate & Explain

Only when you have learned can you evaluate

Only when you have evaluated can you explain

Chapter 7

E = Evaluate and Explain

Whenever you are in a conversation or a discussion with a customer you always need to listen attentively. One reason why you need to listen is you need to evaluate the conversation and the customer.

Ask yourself: is the customer mentioning anything that would make it seem like he or she did not understand something about your product? Is the customer in fact voicing out a concern?

If at any time you find that the customer is mentioning something and you feel that you need to explain further, do so.

You will need to understand that no matter how good you are at explaining something, the customer may have a different method of understanding and your explanation may have been understood with a different meaning.

It is important that the customer fully understands what you are trying to explain, especially if it is about the product. You can never mislead a customer intentionally or unintentionally. If the customer did not understand, you will need to clarify.

If you did not clarify, the way the customer understood what you said may create concerns in the customer's mind. This is a dangerous situation as some of these concerns may not be voiced by the customer and you will end up losing a sale. You always need to evaluate the situation, look for misunderstandings and clarify before you move on.

Create a Powerful Message

While you are evaluating the conversation, look for opportunities where you can create a powerful message. This message has to be able to influence the customer's buying decision.

In the scenario above, your message would be that the car was specifically engineered to be safe. Safety is a priority to the manufacturers. Your message needs to be very clear.

Now, when it comes to messages, it really doesn't matter how they are delivered as long as they are delivered clearly. You can deliver the message verbally or visually. You can show a video you have on file on safety tests of the vehicle if you have one. You can backup your claim by showing safety ratings from a respected safety organization. It doesn't matter how you deliver your message, just make sure that it is powerful and it is clear. Remember that it has to solve a customer's concern so that it can influence the customer's buying decision.

Be Accountable

As a sales person you are accountable for whatever you mentioned to the customer. Do not try to create a powerful message that could actually mislead the customer. Don't say that the vehicle was at the top of the safety ratings when in fact it was near the bottom.

This is the reason why you need to know everything about your product. You need to know its strengths and weaknesses. You need to know its selling points so you can lead the conversation.

However, if the conversation does lead to the weaknesses of the product you are selling do not make it look as if you were avoiding the topic. Every product has a weakness. There is no such thing as a perfect product.

Now, every product has its strengths as well. All you need to do is to find a way to lead the conversation back to the strengths of the product without undermining the customer's concerns about the weakness of your product.

Carefully evaluate the conversation as it moves along. If the conversation is leading to an undesired territory, carefully nudge it back.

If the conversation gets to the point where you are discussing the weaknesses of the product, make sure that you are specific and as honest as possible. If your product was not totally safe, it wouldn't be sold.

Being honest and specific about the weakness of your product does not mean that you have to put your product into bad light.

Provide Solutions to the Exact Concern ONLY!

When you are evaluating the customer's concerns, make sure that you answer the exact concern ONLY! You need to be specific, but do not over explain.

Over explaining may lead to very undesirable scenarios. First, your explanation could bring forth new concerns. Second, the customer may lose focus on buying.

Over explaining is the same as over selling. What exactly does over selling mean? How will you know that you are already over selling?

Over selling is when the customer is sold and willing to buy, but you keep on trying to sell. Every sales person knows not to oversell, but for some reason so many still do. When you over sell, you make your job so much harder than what it really has to be.

There are two reasons why a sales person oversells:

1) The sales person enjoys explaining

2) The sales person does not know when to stop selling

When you start to learn how to hold a real sales conversation, it actually becomes enjoyable. The feeling of being able to convince another person is so strong, that some sales people just can't stop talking. If you listen to this type of conversation, you'll actually find it a bit funny how the sales person is still trying to convince the customer when the customer is already agreeing to everything that the sales person is saying.

The sales person just does not know when to stop selling. What the sales person is waiting for is for the customer to say, "Here's my check, give me the contract and I'll sign it". How ridiculous does that sound?

Well, you might be thinking, how could that possibly sound ridiculous when the sales person just made a sale?

It's like a scene in a movie where a guy keeps on talking trying to court a girl and the girl suddenly kisses him. Okay, well, it may look like its romantic in a movie, but in a sales situation, it just isn't right.

The customer does not need to tell you that he or she is buying your product. If it gets to that point, you've already over sold.

If you over sell you are not doing your job properly. You are not looking for buying signals and you are not doing trial closes. You focused on providing a solution to the customer's concerns so much that you over explained and forgot to look for buying signals and do a trial close.

Now, the whole scenario went fine because the customer ended up buying the product. What if, the result of over explaining went the other way? What if the customer reached a point where he or she was convinced and ready to buy the product, but because you kept on talking, you mentioned another thing that brought up another concern, or worse, got the customer upset?

You ended up losing the sale because you kept on explaining.

This happens a lot of times and some sales people do not even know it. They're thinking that they lost the sale because they weren't able to convince the customer or provide a solution to the customer's concerns, when in fact, they would have gotten the sale if they did their job properly.

As a sales person, you should always keep in mind that you need to listen to the concern, solve it, make sure that the customer is satisfied, and move to a trial close.

Chapter 8

S = Sign & Seal the Deal

Reaching for your goal is not enough

You need to grab it!

Chapter 8

S = Sign & Seal the Deal

Closing is an area that many sales people have trouble with. Some of them simply do not know when to sign and seal the deal. It is not often that you will get into a situation where the customer will actually tell you to pull out the contract so it can be signed. In fact, this rarely happens. If this does happen to you, you know that you missed quite a lot of buying signals.

Closing starts from day one or the very first moment you met the customer. Remember this and you will save yourself a lot of time plus increase your sales.

In the previous chapters we talked about not selling to a person who is already sold. As a salesperson, you need to know when to stop selling and start closing. You need to be able to identify the buying signals and once you do, immediately move for a trial close.

The best sales people want to find out the customer's concern as soon as possible. If the customer does not have any concern, then the closing starts. If the customer does have a concern a solution is provided and the closing starts.

As a sales person, you should always move for a close. How do you know when to close?

The biggest problem that sales people have is that they do not know when to close the deal and they keep wondering when to close the deal, when in fact, the time to close the deal is NOW.

There are many sales people who seemingly have a problem with asking for a check, a signature on a contract, or a firm commitment from their customer. The best sales people always ask. They may not ask directly for a check or a contract signature, but the way they do it means the same thing.

Ask for the business

The most important part about closing is being prepared for a close. In many cases, a close is a simple handshake. If a contract needs to be drafted to the specifications of the customer, ask when you can deliver the contract. If you are to deliver a product, ask when and where it can be delivered. All you need to do is ask.

There's a story about a poor gentleman who really didn't have much going for him. He was working odd jobs all of his life whenever he could find one. He came from a poor family so he couldn't afford an education.

However, he was a deeply religious man. He would pray every night for the good lord to grant him a win in the lottery so that his life would change.

He kept on praying every single night until the very end. When he got to heaven, he faced the lord and asked him why he never won the lottery. He was a good man all his life and he made sure of that because he believed that his faith was the answer to his financial problems.

The lord said, well good man, I granted you a win in the lottery so many times, but you just wouldn't buy a lottery ticket.

As sales people, this happens to us so many times. Not the lottery part, but in getting the business. There are so many sales that we could have closed, but because we didn't do our part and ask, we didn't get the business.

All you need to do is ask. That's what the customer is waiting for. If you're selling, SELL!

Selling is asking for the business. You want the customer to buy so tell the customer to buy.

If someone walks up behind you, pokes something at your back and tells you to hand over your money, you would probably hand it over as fast as you could. Now, if that same person decided to just hold a conversation with you and tell you his or her sad story, would you think of handing over your wallet?

If you're not hitting your sales targets yet you have hundreds of even thousands of prospects, maybe the reason is because you aren't asking for the business.

Whenever you notice a buying signal, ask for the business. There's no harm in asking. If the customer isn't ready to buy yet, there could still be another concern that you need to solve. Provide a solution to that concern and ask for the business again.

In many cases, a sales presentation will look like this:

Presentation

Trial Close

Concerns -> provide solution

Trial Close

Concerns -> provide solution

Trial Close

$OLD or Not sold

Every time you complete a presentation do a trial close. Every time you provide a solution to a concern, do a trial close. There are some excellent sales people, especially those in showrooms, who can close a deal without even having to go through a presentation.

Have you ever gone to an electronic appliances store and you were just looking at a product and the sales person comes up to you and asks if he or she could bring out the product so you can test it? That was a trial close already. The product that will be brought out will be the one that will be delivered to your house or wherever you need it delivered. That's the next question the sales person will ask you.

Now, if you are wondering why the sales person came up to you and asked you directly if a brought could be brought out for you to test. That sales person would probably have been watching you the moment you walked into the store.

Your body language alone could have been buying signals that the sales person detected and that is why the product was offered immediately.

If you noticed, the trial close came even before the presentation. If you agreed to test the product, the sale was already 90% completed. If not, the sales person would move to a presentation and then ask if you would like to test the product. If you had concerns, the sales person would address these concerns and then move for a trial close again.

Always remember that selling is closing. Make your sale the least complicated as possible by closing it immediately or whenever you can.

How to Recognize Buying Signals

What are buying signals and how do you recognize them? Buying signals are indications that your customer is at the brink of buying. When a customer starts to give out buying signals, this means that the customer has already made up his or her mind to buy. All you need to do is to give your customer a little push and your product is sold.

Once you are able to identify any buying signal, it is your cue to do a trial closing. It is important that you don't wait. Go for the close right then and there because the chances are high that you will get the deal.

When a customer gives out a buying signal, stop selling. If you keep on selling, you run the risk of the customer having a change of heart and the deal will slip through your fingers.

The following are common buying signals that you will need to watch out for:

When the customer starts talking about ownership

Do you remember the example in the previous chapters of how a customer would start talking about how the kids or other family members would love this and that portion of a house you were selling? Now, the customer did not exactly mention that he or she wanted to buy the house, but the customer's words indicated that they were already imagining owning the property. This is a strong buying signal and you should immediately act to close the deal.

Don't go showing other areas of the property saying that you're sure that the kids would love this and that too. You're over selling if you do this. All you need to do is to ask your customer when he or she would like to sign the paperwork. This is a trial close.

The customer may give you a date or may ask for further information about the price or payment terms. That's fine because this is another buying signal.

When the customer starts talking about payment or money matters

It's a done deal when the customer starts talking about payment terms. If the customer starts to bargain or starts looking for easier payment terms, the customer has already made up in his mind that he wants to buy. There is a good chance that the customer already likes the product but just wants to see if a better deal can be reached.

As a sales person you will always want to go for a win-win situation. You want your customers to have the best deal, yet you also need to make sure that you and the company that you represent also get a good deal.

In most cases, your company will have already a certain price range that you can play with. In some cases, the company may be able to offer easier payment terms.

Before you ever start a sales process, make sure that you know what offers you can give to your customers. You surely won't want to start offering the best offer. Always leave yourself a little room for negotiation. Many customers, in fact most customers, already know that there is always room for negotiations. These customers will want to negotiate and if you don't leave yourself room for negotiations, you will most likely lose the sale.

When you make decisions for the customer and the customer agrees

There can be times when a customer can't seem to make a choice or a decision about a product. When this happens, you can make a suggestion. If the customer agrees, then this is a strong buying signal.

Immediately go for a trial close because the sale is almost completed.

Putting words into the customer's mouth will sometimes work, especially if you've already been able to establish rapport. However, you should be careful when applying this tactic as some customers prefer to make-up their own minds. They do not want to feel like being lead to a decision.

The key to closing a sale fast is to do a trail close whenever you identify a buying signal. Don't be afraid to do a trial close and don't hesitate. A buying signal is an indication that the customer is ready to buy and all the customer is waiting for is you to offer the deal and close it. If for some reason the customer hesitates after you do a trial close, find out what the concern is and provide a solution.

Once you provide a solution that is acceptable to the client, you will most likely see another buying signal and you need to do another trial close. Keep on doing trial closes whenever you see the chance. Always keep in mind that there is no harm in trying to seal the deal as long as you see that the customer is ready for it.

Chapter 9

Developing Conversational Skills

A conversation is made up to two parts: Listening & Expressing

Knowing when to listen and when to express is the problem

Chapter 9

Developing Conversational Skills

If you've been paying close attention to the S.A.L.E.S = $OLD sales presentation model, you will have noticed that the key ingredient to a successful selling career is having the ability to hold a meaningful conversation with the customer.

Keep in mind that you are a sales person and that your job is to sell whatever product your company wants you to sell. In some cases, you'll get lucky and close a deal without much of an effort, but you can't rely on this happening all the time. Most of the time, you'll be working hard for your money. How hard you work and how much you actually sell will depend on your conversational skills as a sales person.

Before we continue, are you the type of person who can hold a conversation with just about anybody? Do you find it easy to walk up to someone, introduce yourself, and start having a good conversation?

The answers to both of those questions should be yes. If you have any fears whatsoever about approaching a total stranger and start having a conversation, then you should start developing your conversational skills immediately. Without these skills, you will not progress in your career.

Now, you can find plenty of books about developing conversational skills, but the skills you need to develop are those needed by a sales person. In sales, whenever you have a conversation with anybody, you have only one objective and that is to make a sale. Every time you talk to anybody, you should be laying the ground works or the foundation for a sale. Why?

You need to focus on making a sale every time you talk with someone simply because you need to establish your reputation as a sales person. Before you can sell your product, you need to sell yourself.

You need to become the go-to guy. Whenever anyone you spoke to in the past thinks about or has a need for the product you are selling, you want to be the person that that person thinks of. If there is someone that they know who needs your product, you should be the person that they refer.

The only way you can do this is by building a reputation. How many other sales people have you met in the past and actually remembered their names or the products they were selling? Now, ask yourself, why did you remember their names and their products?

You may just have an extremely good memory, or it will likely be because that person had a conversation with you that you remembered.

As a sales person, everybody needs to be able to remember your name. If you are successful in building your reputation, you'll find that sales won't be so difficult anymore. In time, you will notice that you're spending fewer hours looking for prospects and more hours closing deals.

As a sales professional, you will most likely have developed your own style of approaching your customers and holding a conversation with them. Now, do you use the same style with all of your customers? If you do, then you probably would have noticed that you find it easier dealing with some people and a bit harder dealing with others. You will also have noticed that you can close more sales with the people that you find it easier to deal with.

However, spend a minute to think about the sales that you lost or weren't able to close. Do you think that there may have been a little bit of personality issues between you and the customer? One of the most popular reasons why a sale wasn't closed was because of personality differences between the sales person and the customer.

Most, if not all of sales professionals have undergone several training sessions on how to handle customer objections. Unfortunately, there aren't many training sessions on how to avoid customer objections.

If you can hold a conversation in such a way that you can actually limit the objections, then you'll most likely have more sales. The key to avoiding objections from coming up is having the ability to understand the customer.

Understanding the customer is one of the most important aspects of sales. Sales professionals need to be able to understand their customers in order to hold meaningful conversations that will lead to a sale.

However, before you even attempt to understand other people, you will first need to understand yourself. What type of person are you? How do other people perceive you? Do other people see you as the person you really are or are you projecting a different type of personality?

In the earlier chapters we talked about DISC profiling. Here we go into this method a little bit deeper because this is what you will need to develop your conversational skills. We will first analyze what quadrant your personality falls into. Once you understand your own personality, you'll know how your customers perceive you.

Here are the quadrants again so you don't have to flip back and look for the meaning.

D = Dominance

I = Influence

S = Steadiness

C = Compliance

Sit back for a minute and ask yourself which quadrant you fall into.

Are you the dominant type of person? Dominant people have very strong personalities. They are independent, decisive, and very strong-willed. If you have this type of personality, you will likely find it a bit difficult to see other people's opinions, mainly because you are focused on your own opinion.

You also find a need to be in control of every situation. Not being in control can be a bit upsetting so you find ways to assert yourself until you have control.

Becoming a sales person with a dominant personality can be a bit difficult because your personality may be too strong for some customers. However, if you learn how to quickly identify the personality of your customers, you can adjust your own personality.

The Dominant Sales Person

If you're a sales person with a dominant personality, you'll find it easy to hold a conversation with a customer who has the same personality. You are naturally direct whenever you speak and this is important to dominant customers.

You will naturally be aggressive because of your competitive nature. However, it would be best to control your aggressiveness with customers. You need to know exactly when you can be aggressive and produce positive results. There are times when being too aggressive can produce negative results.

It is crucial that you learn how to read the personalities of your customers so you know when you can be aggressive and when to hold back a little.

Dominant Sales Person with a Dominant Customer

Dominant customers are demanding. They know exactly what they want and enjoy intimidating a sales person.

The dominant customer is also very direct. They want to know what is being offered and how whatever it is can be beneficial to them. Dominant customers always want the best deal. If they can be convinced that they are receiving the best offer, then they can be quick to make a decision.

As a dominant sales person, you should not have any problems with being direct. You know exactly what you can or can not provide to the customer. If there is something that your company is unable to provide, make sure that you offer alternatives.

If you have a dominant personality, you will find it a bit comforting to not have to go into too many details. Like you, dominant customers do not want to go into details. They are focused on the bottom line and this is where most of their concerns will come from.

Customers with dominant personalities do not like being told what to do. In fact, it's the other way around. A dominant customer will try to direct the terms. They will come up with situations where the sales person has to accept those terms or the customer will choose another company to purchase from.

A sales person with a dominant personality will be less intimidated by the tactics used by dominant customers. In fact, a dominant customer will be less likely to apply intimidation tactics to a dominant sales person.

Dominant Sales Person with Influence Customer

Customers who have the Influence personality are naturally talkative. They love to express themselves so they are naturally friendly in order to gain an audience.

Unfortunately, as a dominant sales person, you may find it to be a bit irritating to be talking to customers under the Influence quadrant. They love to talk but they don't listen very attentively. This is one of the reasons why they will likely be asking the same question more than once. You will need to be a bit patient because there will be times when you'll need to explain over and over again.

With a dominant personality, you will naturally be a bit impatient and you will most likely show a bit of disinterest in what a customer with an influence personality is saying, especially when the customer jumps from topic to topic.

You will also likely be a bit disappointed when the customer pays little attention to what you are saying. Instead of showing your disappointment, try to find a way to get the customer to be more attentive.

With a dominant personality, you won't be welcome to distractions. You would rather be sitting in a closed office with your customer to limit the amount of distractions. However, customers with the influence personality are a bit lively. They welcome multi-tasking and as such they entertain distractions. It would be best to expect interruptions. Just pick up from the point of the interruption when you can get back on the topic.

Dominant Sales Person to Customer with Steadiness Personality

Customers who have this personality are the easiest ones to get along with, especially for sales people with dominant personalities. These customers are very relaxed and they are very attentive as well. They listen very carefully and they analyze every bit of the conversation.

It can be a bit difficult to quickly close a deal with these customers as they are slow to making a decision. However, your dominant personality will help you guide the customer into making a decision in your favor or to come to a conclusion that you want.

Customers with this type of personality are logical so as long as you can make them see the logic in something it will not be difficult in having a conversation with them.

You will also need to keep in mind that these customers are not very emotional. It can be a bit difficult for them to voice out their true concerns and this is why they won't make quick decisions.

At times during your conversation with them, you may get the feeling that there is something that they are concerned about. With your personality, you're used to being direct and you will voice out your concerns. Unfortunately this type of customer will not act in the same way.

If you do get the feeling that your customer is concerned about something, the customer probably is. You will need to ask questions to find out what they are really concerned about.

Dominant Sales Person to Customer with Compliance Personality

Customers under this category tend to be a bit more careful on their purchases. They normally want to be aware of all the details so that they can study them and make a decision.

These customers may seem to be a bit reserved when in front of someone with a dominant personality. You will have to tone down your personality a little bit when having a conversation with them.

One good thing about this type of personality is that it isn't very hard to hold a conversation with them. They are very interested in the details so they have a tendency to ask quite a lot of questions. It is best to answer the questions with facts in order to help this customer make a purchasing decision.

When having a conversation with this type of customer, keep in mind that they may not agree with what you are saying but they often won't tell you. This can become a bit of a problem when trying to provide solutions to their concerns.

You will need to ask them a lot of open-ended questions to get them to open up at first. They will be happy to answer closed-ended questions but you may not get very far in terms of finding out their true feelings.

Keep in mind that these customers have almost the opposite personality so you will need to be careful not to scare them away. Try to be less commanding. It would be better to listen and keep on encouraging this type of person to talk. The more they talk, the more information you are likely to get that you can use to assess his or her concerns.

Another thing to remember is that these customers love paying close attention to details. With a dominant personality, you will have a tendency to not focus too much on details. Unfortunately, you will have to be as detailed as you can be in order to have a meaningful conversation with these customers.

Sales persons under the Influence quadrant

Sales people with this type of personality can be considered as naturals. You do not find it difficult to make customers feel at ease with your personality thus you can create rapport rather quickly.

With this type of personality, you are naturally energetic and enthusiastic in the way you deliver your presentation. Your energy and enthusiasm will play a big part in convincing your customers.

Influence Sales Persons to Dominant Customers

You will need to remember that dominant customers have less time for small talk. They want to get right down to the facts so that they can make decisions. With dominant customers, you will need to be a little bit less talkative so focus more on the subject.

It is your nature to be very accommodating. You love to entertain customers and will have a tendency to greet anybody who comes by you. Now, this can present a bit of a problem with dominant customers as they want your full attention. In fact, they will most likely demand that you stay focused on your conversation with them instead of saying hi or hello to everyone who passes by.

Your talkative nature will make you want to come up with lengthy explanations about a certain subject. Try to avoid these lengthy explanations and get direct to the point. Keep in mind that dominant personalities do not have time to go into all of the details. They want to know exactly they are to receive and when they are going to receive it. It will not matter to them how you are going to deliver, as long as you can assure them that your delivery will be on time.

You will need to careful in the way you hold the conversation as not to go with your tendency to jump from topic to topic. A dominant customer will not want to keep up with you if you do this. They prefer to stick to a topic until it has been resolved before moving on to another one.

As a sales person with the influence personality, you can think pretty quickly. However, there may come times when you might lose focus on what the customer is saying because you're thinking of the next thing to say. Dominant customers want other people to listen attentively to what they are saying. You will need to hold back a little on talking and focus more on listening with this type of customer.

Whenever you have a dominant customer, do not interrupt. There are times when you have the tendency to finish other people's sentences. Unless this type of customer asks you for the best word to finish the sentence, do not offer your opinion. The customer may be thinking of another word and your interruption may not be welcome.

Influence Sales Persons to Influence Customers

When you're having a conversation to a customer that has the same personality, you'll find that the conversation will be enjoyable. You'll go into details and most likely be discussing things that are not even related to your sale.

It is easy for you to build rapport, but in doing so, you might take the risk of spending too much time on unnecessary topics. Remember that you will need to keep the conversation under control. It would be best to use your natural ability to talk to keep the conversation from wondering on to different topics. Always be prepared with alternatives so you can lead the conversation to discussing these instead of something that has nothing to do with your product.

You will also have the tendency to over sell with this type of customer, especially if you get into lengthy conversations. The best thing to do is to focus on watching for buying signals. Whenever you customer displays a buying signal, go straight for a trial close. Once you close the deal, it really won't matter how much you want to continue talking with your customer. It will actually do you good to build up a relationship as this can lead to future sales.

Influence Sales Persons to Customers under the Steadiness Quadrant

Your natural ability to talk may overwhelm this type of customer if you do not stick to the topic. Keep in mind that these customers are a bit more focused on details so that they can make their decisions. If you talk about too many different things, the customer may lose focus and not want to buy.

Another thing that you should remember is that this type of customer wants to hear and discuss even the negative aspects of your product. Though it is advisable not to go into lengthy conversations about the negative aspects, do not try to avoid it as well.

You will need to develop your listening skills in order to hold a meaningful conversation with this type of customer. They may not talk often, but you should listen to them when they do. It would be a good point to let them finish what they have to say without any interruptions. Just be patient and listen attentively.

This type of customer will also not be able to make quick decisions. You may have to help them a bit in this aspect, but be careful in the way you lead them to a decision. They do not want to be hurried because they want to be perfectly sure that they are making the right decision.

Always keep in mind that this type of customer thinks logically. They prefer to feel at ease with a certain topic before moving on. Your tendency to jump from one topic to another will not be welcomed with this type of customer. Make sure that the customer is satisfied with one topic first before you move on to another.

Influence Sales Persons and Compliant Customers

One of your best assets is your natural energy and your enthusiasm, but you might just be too energetic and enthusiastic around compliant customers. This type of customer likes to take things slowly. They have a need to study information closely before they can move on.

Whenever you're having a conversation with this type of customer, try to avoid talking too fast or presenting information too quickly. You will need to understand that compliant customers are focused on details. While you have no problem with presenting details, you do have the tendency to present them way too fast for this type of customer.

When you're presenting the details of your product, make sure that the customer understands one detail before you move on.

This type of customer will most likely ask quite a lot of questions about your product. Now, you can be sure that they will most likely have done a bit of research before your presentation and if what you are saying differs from their research they will be asking questions until they are satisfied that they understand.

Compliant customers have a tendency to be a bit reserved. You can't expect them to be as lively as you when it comes to a conversation. It would be best to make an attempt to get them to open up a bit more.

They prefer to talk about the details and specifications of your product without really showing much emotion as to whether or not they want to buy it. It can be a bit difficult to look for buying signals because of their lack of emotion, but there will be some if you listen attentively to what they are saying.

The Steadiness Type of Sales Person

This type of personality enables you to be calm and focused which is why you are a good listener. You can easily gain a customer's trust because customers will perceive you as being a trustworthy individual. However, you have a tendency of not being able to talk too much and this may come as a bit of a problem when you're facing customers who want to be entertained.

One of your strongest skills is asking open-ended questions to encourage the customer to talk mainly so that you can listen. This is a good strategy for some customers, but other customers may find you to be a bit boring so you need to be careful and know when you need to talk to entertain your customer.

Steadiness Sales Person and Dominant Customers

One of your strengths in a conversation with a dominant customer is your ability to think logically and express yourself the same way. However, you need to remember that dominant people will be more focused on how they will benefit from your product. They are less concerned about how your product benefits the general population and more focused on how they as an individual will benefit from it.

Dominant customers have a tendency to be blunt and very direct. They say what they want without even considering how it may affect the other person.

Fortunately, you have a very calm personality and you are not easily rattled.

Whenever you're having a conversation with a dominant customer, keep in mind that you need to get to the bottom line as quick as you can. It would be best to start by describing how your product with benefit your customer and then provide some support as to how you came to that conclusion.

Steadiness Sales Person and Influence Customers

Influence customers will really give you a challenge because you will need to talk more often. You are a great listener, but customers under this quadrant also like people who they can hold a conversation with. Influence customers are enthusiastic and energetic so you will need to match their enthusiasm.

It is in your nature to ask open-ended questions to encourage conversation, but with influence customers, you won't need to be asking too many open-ended questions. In fact, you may have a bit of a problem if you do. It would be better to lead the conversation by asking closed-ended questions to give you the opportunity to talk.

Your listening skills will help you keep up with this type of customer as they love to jump from topic to topic. Listen carefully and look for opportunities where you can do a trial close.

A customer with this type of personality may be jumping from topic to topic but there will always be an underlying reason. Your listening skills will help you identify this reason and assess the customer a bit more carefully.

Showing your enthusiasm in the conversation will be your biggest challenge, but if you can overcome this, it will be easy for you to close a sale with this type of customer.

Steadiness Sales Person and Steadiness Customer

Have you ever had the opportunity to listen to a conversation between two enthusiastic people? The conversation will be lively with each person offering views and opinions. Now, this is quite different from a conversation between two calm individuals. In fact, this type of conversation can be a bit boring because each one wants to listen more than talk.

Unfortunately, you will find yourself in this situation when you meet a customer with the same personality as yours. Try to avoid "dead air" or moments when neither of you are talking. Always be ready to offer your opinion when you ask for your customer's opinion because this type of customer will likely ask for it.

Like you, this type of customer also has excellent listening skills so make sure that you stick with facts all throughout your conversation. You will also need to become pro-active and encourage a discussion. Make an extra effort to show enthusiasm and be a bit more energetic. You are naturally calm, but in this situation, you will need to be a bit more enthusiastic to encourage your customer to talk.

Steadiness Sales Person and Compliant Customer

Compliant customers have a tendency to ask a lot of questions and your natural ability to stay calm will allow you to answer those questions as direct as possible. Keep in mind that you need to be direct and stick to the facts. You will also be good in explaining details as this type of customer needs information to make a buying decision.

You will need to be lively and a bit enthusiastic, but don't overdo it. Compliant customers don't really want to encourage a discussion because all they are really concerned about are the details.

This type of customer will make you do a lot of talking by asking you questions on the details of your product. You may not be naturally talkative, but that won't matter because you will be explaining your product. However, do make an effort to create a more lively conversation. Try to get the customer involved in a conversation by asking questions about his or her opinion.

The Compliant Sales Person

People with compliant personalities tend to be more focused on the details rather than just looking at the wide picture. Sales people with this type of personality usually know a lot about their products and can hold lengthy conversations on the details alone.

Product knowledge is crucial in a sales presentation and this is the type of sales person you can rely on to focus on the details. However, as you know product knowledge is not enough to close a deal. It may play a big part in the presentation, but creating rapport and effective closing techniques are also needed to seal the deal.

One of the biggest problems of sales people with this personality is that they find it difficult to hold conversations with their customers. They are good at explaining the details of their products, but have a bit of a problem when trying to lead a conversation.

In order to lead a conversation a sales person needs to be a bit energetic, enthusiastic, and assertive. A compliant sales person has a tendency to be a bit quiet and a bit cautious as well.

Compliant sales people need to focus less on presenting the details of the product and more on creating an attachment with the customer. A sales presentation that is focused on the product and not on the customer is bound for failure.

It's fine to present the details as long as these are presented in such a way that they provide solutions to a particular customer concern. However, the sales person needs to identify the customer's concerns first before he or she can provide a solution. The best way to find out what these concerns are is to first create rapport and the sales person needs to be a skilful conversationalist to do this.

Because of their personality, compliant sales people will need to work harder on developing their conversational skills.

The Compliant Sales Person and the Dominant Customer

When presenting to a dominant customer, a compliant sales person will need to be assertive. They need to find out exactly what the customer wants and provide a solution as fast as they possibly can.

The sales person will also need to keep in mind that focusing on the details of a product will not work with a dominant customer. This type of customer does not want to get into the details. All they are looking for is for a product that will provide a solution to their problems. If the sales person keeps going into the details, this customer will likely get a bit impatient.

Dominant customers are normally not the technical type of people so it would be futile to go into an in depth technical analysis of your product. Just be prepared to discuss the selling points or the strongest points about your product and how these will solve the concerns of the customer.

A compliant sales person can also be a bit cautious when applying closing techniques. Being hesitant to ask for the business will not work with a dominant customer. Aggressive closing strategies need to be applied to dominant customers. If you are able to provide solutions to their concerns, go for a trial close.

Dominant customers have a tendency to make quick decisions so you need to be aggressive when asking for their business. However, keep in mind that you need to provide a solution first or the dominant customer will be quick to reject your product as well.

The Compliant Sales Person and the Influence Customer

The biggest problem that you will have with influence customers is that they love to talk. You on the other hand, really don't want to do a lot of talking outside of topics like details and processes. Influence customers may find you to be a little bit boring if the conversation isn't about your product.

Another thing that influence customers love doing is playing around with the rules. They're not too big on rules, regulations and processes which is quite the opposite of your personality. However, you need to be a bit flexible when having a conversation with this type of customer.

Always know before hand what your limitations are and if you can stretch them a little. For example: Your customer playfully asks you for a 12% discount but you know that the company is only offering up to 10%.You should also know if your company is willing to offer a bit more and most companies usually do. If the limit of your company is only up to 11%, you can use this to close the sale by asking for commitment if you agree to give up to 11%. This type of customer only wanted you to stretch the limit a bit further and by agreeing to stretch it a little bit you practically closed the sale already.

The Compliant Sales Person and the Steadiness Customer

Customers who fall under this category are usually calm and logical. You can use this to your advantage as you have a passion for details and processes. However, try to explain each step as clearly as possible. Try to avoid getting mixed up as this type of customer does not want confusion.

You may find yourself getting a bit too excited by getting the opportunity to explain details and processes but you may end up doing so in such a way that it can confuse the customer.

Always ask this type of customer for an opinion but be prepared to come up with a meaningful discussion. This means that you need to present some examples so you need to be prepared.

The Compliant Sales Person and the Compliant Customer

This is the best type of customer for your personality. The both of you love going into discussions about details and facts so you won't have much of a problem keeping the customer interested. However, your excitement may overshadow the customer so be careful.

Keep in mind that compliant customers are naturally quiet until the part where the conversation gets into the details of the product. This is when they will start to ask questions and the conversation will get a bit more interesting. However, before this happens it can be a bit difficult to create rapport so you need to be lively right from the very start.

It would be best to encourage this type of customer to talk more by asking open-ended questions that will require the customer to provide an opinion. Be prepared to provide your own opinions so you can keep the conversation flowing in a lively manner.

When it comes to closing the sale, the compliant customer may seem a bit cautious when committing to a purchase. You will normally be able to get a commitment after the customer has been able to carefully study the details. This won't be a problem to you because you'll find it easy to discuss the details.

However, look carefully for buying signals so you can attempt a trial close. This type of customer won't offer many buying signals so it would be best to lead the conversation in such a way that the customer will have to give you a buying signal or come up with another concern.

The basic conversational strategy for all types of customers

Adapting to a customer's personality can be a bit difficult, especially if the customer has a personality that is the exact opposite of yours. However, if you want to become one of the best sales persons you will need to learn to adapt sooner or later.

If you are unsure of whether or not you can adapt to a personality, then here are a few tips that you can do. These are easy to remember and will work for any type of personality.

Be enthusiastic but sincere – Nobody wants a dull conversation. As a salesperson you need to show enthusiasm or your customer may quickly lose interest in the product that you are selling. However, be careful not to sound over enthusiastic like the voices of those presenters you can hear on the shopping channel.

Becoming over enthusiastic can somehow give the impression that you lack sincerity. If you are over enthusiastic, your customer will think that you are desperate to get the business. The key to becoming enthusiastic is becoming sincere. The first thing that customers will always look for is sincerity and they can tell if you are sincere or not just by the way you talk.

Ask for the customer's opinion – regardless of what type of personality you are dealing with, always ask for an opinion. Keep in mind that some customers may not want to give an opinion if the topic is too general. For example: if you ask a customer what he or she thinks about the car you are selling, some customers may just nod, smile and reply with "it looks fine". On the other hand, if you ask the customer about his or her opinion about the color of the car, then you will likely be able to gauge the color preferences of the customer.

When asking for an opinion, try to be a bit more specific. Customers will usually have an opinion on a specific topic instead of a general one.

Respect the customer's opinion – whatever the customer's opinion is, make sure that you show your respect. In sales, keep in mind that you will most likely be dealing with not only different personalities, but with different cultures as well.

Not everybody you will meet in your line of work will have the same beliefs as yours. There are topics that you would be better off staying away from. Topics like religion and politics may be good conversational topics between friends, but discussing these with a total stranger may work against you. However, if these topics do come up, make sure that you respect the person's opinion and try to steer the conversation back to the products you are offering.

Avoid Dead Air – Unless the customer is taking a moment to think, avoid dull moments where neither of you is speaking. You should always find something to talk about and the best topic is about your product. In situations where you can't seem to think of something to say, it is best to ask a question. You can either ask for the customer's opinion on a certain aspect of your product, or you can ask the customer about ways he or she perceives the product to be helpful.

Always make it a point to strive to keep the conversation lively. You need to gain the interest of the customer in order for the customer to make a buying decision. Once you develop your conversational skills, you'll be able to quickly find out exactly what the customer needs and how your product can satisfy those needs.

Make an attempt to close the deal – Plenty of sales professionals are good conversationalists but they have a tendency to forget that closing the deal is the primary objective. There will always be an opportunity to close if you watch for them. Now, if you can't get a firm purchasing commitment from the customer, at least try to establish a date for another meeting. You will need to be persistent in this line of work. There will be times when sales just do not come easy and you'll need to work very hard.

Chapter 10

Planning the Sale

Living without a plan is not living; it is known as existing

Chapter 10

Planning the Sale

The importance of planning and preparation can often be overlooked by many sales professionals. In fact, there have been plenty of circumstances where sales have been lost simply because the sales professional failed to plan and prepare.

Every customer is a deal waiting to happen and if you don't keep this in mind, chances are you'll be ill prepared to close deals. You need to be prepared every single time you meet with a customer. Do not let a deal slip through your fingers because you weren't prepared.

In order to successfully apply the S.A.L.E.S = $OLD sales process, you need to carefully plan and prepare for your sales call. Every stage in this process is designed so that you can provide specific directions and objectives to your sales call.

Here are some tips on how to plan and prepare for a sales call.

Know your product

This may seem rather obvious, but actually, it isn't. Surprisingly, there are so many sales professionals who fail to update themselves with the product they are selling. For example, you set a sales call with a client a couple of days from now. You've got quite a number of sales calls before then and you're busy attending to every one of them. Unfortunately, your company rolls out some changes in the product and you failed to read the memo of the changes.

Keep in mind that customers generally do not want to be surprised at sudden changes. If you present one thing, make sure that it is exactly what you're going to deliver.

What if you make a sale, but there were changes to the product? How would you convince the customer to agree to those changes? It will not be easy and the customer may just back away from the sale.

Always know before hand if you can deliver the product you are presenting. Make it a point to check for availability or any changes in product specifications. These are the two areas that many sales professionals fail to get updates on.

Know your customer

How much research have you done on your customer? It is not enough to simply know the name and title of the person. The more information you can get the better. If you are going to be presenting to a company, make sure that you familiarize yourself with the company profile. It will be a good idea to find information about how the company's business has been doing the past months or years.

How will your product help this company? What are the strengths of your product that you believe will enable you to close the sale? Is there anything about your product that your competitors do not have? These are questions that you should have answers to before you head for that sales call. Knowing the right answers to those questions will enable you to focus the conversation on the strengths of your product.

Define your objectives

Every sales call must have an objective and the sales person must work to achieve it. The objective may or may not include closing the deal on that particular call. Whatever your objectives are, you will need to work to achieve them. The way to achieve them is to direct focus on those objectives.

Remember that a sales call does not have to be complicated. If you have too many objectives, you will likely lose the customer. It would be best to divide your strategy into stages and work on achieving each stage instead of trying to achieve all of your objectives in one sales call.

Initial sales calls may be focused on creating a bond with the customer. The sales call may be focused on fact finding. The sales person can attempt to find out exactly how the products can help the company.

Not every sales call needs to be focused on closing the deal immediately. However, if the opportunity presents itself, there is no reason why the sales person should not attempt a trial close.

Prepare for objections

Objections are a part of every sales call and you should be prepared to handle them. List down all of the possible objections and make sure that you also have your best response.

One of the biggest mistakes of sales professionals is not preparing adequately for objections. When an objection does come up, the sales person is left struggling to quickly find a response. You need to keep in mind that the flow of your conversation with the customer is critical. If the customer gives an objection, you need to be prepared to answer it quickly.

Customers expect you to provide solutions to their problems. If you can't provide solutions, the customer will find another company to deal with.

Now, the only way that you will be able to prepare for the objections is to know the company or the person who you will be dealing with. The more information you can get about the company, the better you can prepare for possible objections.

If you've ever had the opportunity to accompany some of the best sales people on their sales calls, you'll probably be amazed at how fast they can provide solutions to the customer's objections. Don't for a minute think that they are just fast thinkers. The speed in how they can respond to objections is directly related at how much knowledge they have about the customer before hand.

Know your competitors

Knowing your competitors does not mean that you need to showcase their weaknesses in order to build-up your product. What this means is that you need to know their strengths. You can be sure that the customer will know your competitors and will be trying to compare strengths and weaknesses in order to make the right decision.

If you know the strengths of your competitors, you can provide solutions to a customer's objections on your product. There can also be customers who want your product but may attempt to bargain for a better deal by claiming one of your competitors is offering a better price. If you know your competitors then you'll be able to tell if what the customer is saying is true or exaggerated.

Know Yourself

This is the most important part in planning and preparation for sales calls. As a sales person, you need to know yourself. What are your strengths and weaknesses? What type of people can you easily get along with and what type of people make sales calls difficult for you.

Your sales strategy will largely depend on how well you know yourself. It would be useless to attempt at selling to a certain customer when you think you won't be able to close the deal. In such a case, it would be best to enlist the help of your team leader or manager.

The reason why you need the help of someone who can close the deal is so that you can learn. In sales, mistakes results in lost revenue for your company. Mistakes also result in a poor performance record which could ultimately result in you losing your job.

If you know yourself, you know when to ask for assistance. If you ask for help and the deal is closed, you played a part in the success. If you don't ask for help and you fail to close the deal, you will take full responsibility.

Learning from your mistakes can be costly in sales so make sure that you know yourself before you make a sales call.

In the following chapters we will take a closer look at why customers won't buy and how to handle objections. Planning a sale means to understand why a customer won't buy and how the customer will object.

Chapter 11

Why Customers WON'T Buy

Before you sell your product, sell its value

Chapter 11

Why Customers Won't Buy

As a sales person you probably have accounts that you weren't able to seal the deal on. In many cases, you worked hard to get that customer but you failed to get a signed contract. Not all sales calls end up successful. Many sales calls end up as failures, but it is from these failures that we can improve our sales strategies.

It's important that you analyze every sales call, especially the ones that ended up as failures. You need to find out exactly why that call ended up as a failure. Finding out these reasons will help you improve on your future sales calls.

There are many reasons why a sales call can end up as a failure and most of these reasons are because of simple mistakes by the sales person. Let's take a look at some of the common reasons why a customer would not buy.

Lack of Value

When a customer perceives a product to be lacking in value, then the sale will not push through. If a customer fails to see "value" in the product, then it is likely because the sales person was not able to provide a solution to the customer's concerns.

This is why sales people need to listen attentively to a customer's concerns or even probe deeper when necessary. It is imperative that a customer's true concerns are identified so that "value" can be established.

Value can mean different things to a customer but it is usually of these three: Functional, Financial, or Emotional.

Functional value is when your product is needed by the customer as a necessary part of their product. This is common in the manufacturing industry where a product can be made out of several different products by different suppliers. Your product can be a raw material or a particular assembly of a bigger product.

When customers are looking for functional value they usually know exactly what they need. In many cases, they already have specifications that need to be met. As long as these specifications are met or even exceeded, then the product will have functional value.

Functional value can have to do a lot with quality. When a customer needs to sell quality products that customer will naturally need quality materials for their products. If your product has the right quality, then it will likely be considered for purchase.

When it comes to the quality of your product, there's not much you can do as a sales person. You can only sell what your company is producing and you will have no control whatsoever in the quality of the product that your company creates.

It is important to take note that customers don't always consider functional value alone when making their purchasing decisions. Having a high, medium, or low quality product does not necessarily mean that you will win or lose a contract. A customer will usually compare functional value with financial value.

Financial value is when your product will create a positive financial impact to the customer. Your product may reduce the customer's manufacturing or overhead costs. It may reduce the price of a customer's product, or it may increase the value of the customer's product.

Customers need to find out the financial impact of your product. As a sales person you need to find out how your product will benefit your customer financially. You need to find out if your product has the lowest prices in the market or if you can lower it even more. If your product is not exactly the lowest, will it be able to provide other financial benefits.

Quality products tend to be more expensive because they will last longer or have more functions. If you can't provide the lowest prices, maybe your product will be able to create long term savings for your customer.

It really doesn't matter if you're selling the lowest or highest priced products as long as you can convince your customer of its financial value.

Customers also make their purchasing decisions based on emotional value. Emotional value is established when you've been able to create an emotional bond between you and your customer or between your company and your customer.

Trust has a lot to do when it comes to creating emotional value. Many customers are loyal to their suppliers simply because they trust them. In some cases, emotional value will weigh more heavily in a customer's purchasing decisions.

Lack of Urgency

In some cases a customer won't buy because he or she does not see an urgency to purchase your product. As a sales person, you need to be able to create this urgency if at all possible. Why does your customer need to buy your product "now"? Why does the customer need to act?

In many cases sales people fail to create "urgency" when selling their products. Now, creating urgency is a common sales technique used by sales people, but you need to be careful in what technique you use with a customer. Not all techniques will have positive results. In fact, if applied incorrectly a technique like this can backfire.

The best way to create urgency is to do research about your customer and the industry that your customer belongs to. For example: you are selling a petroleum based product and you find out that your customer needs your product to manufacture a product of their own.

Now, your company is predicting a mark-up on the product that you are selling due to a forecasted increase in petroleum prices. However, your company will be able to maintain its prices for an extended limit of time because of the current supplies. In this scenario you can use the urgency technique to sell your product.

Customer perceives your product as being inferior to others

Even the best products may seem inferior to other offerings in the eyes of the customer. Every product has its strengths and weaknesses and this is why it is important for sales people to be familiar with their products.

A product can sometimes be inferior in some ways but superior in others. If the customer is focused on the weaknesses of the product, then you need to bring back the customer's focus on the strengths of your product.

There are many sales people who tend to freeze when it comes to discussions about the weaknesses of their products. It all has to do with your customer's perception of your product as a whole.

There are also many sales people whose products aren't exactly the best there are in the market, but are able to build-up their products in the eyes of the customers. Even inferior products can seem great if you're selling to the right market.

Selling a product that is inferior in quality can be quite difficult if you're selling to the wrong customer. Some customers require high quality products while others may not be that particular with quality.

As a sales person, you need to find out what market you need to be selling to and to focus on that market. Choose your market carefully because you do not want to be spending too much time selling to a market that is least likely to buy your product.

Customers won't always tell you bluntly that your product is inferior to other products being offered. How do you find out if a customer is thinking this but not showing it? It is important that you always ask for the customer's opinion. Some customers will only offer their opinions when asked. If you don't ask, you might not be able to find out the customer's true concerns.

Now, if the customer tells you that your product is considered to be inferior to other products being offered then ask again. Ask for the reason why the customer considers your product to be inferior and you will most likely receive an honest opinion.

Some customers may have the wrong perception because of a misunderstanding. There are customers who do their research about the different products being offered and sometimes their research may not be accurate.

There is also a chance that the customer did not understand your product presentation. You may have said something that made the customer jump to a wrong conclusion. You will not be able to clarify the situation if you don't probe deeper. Always make sure that you understand the exact concerns of the customer.

Internal Office Politics

It is not uncommon to find yourself selling to a company with internal office politics. Almost every company has office politics, some worse than others. Unfortunately, office politics can at times affect the decision making abilities of the company.

A company will usually have two or more decision makers. Even a purchase request will sometimes need to be signed by at the very least two decision makers. The purchase itself will first need to be approved by the procurement manager and then by an even higher company official.

There will be times when all of these decision makers don't see eye to eye. When office politics steps in, some may disagree on a purchase just for the sake of disagreeing with a decision.

As a sales person that sells products to mostly companies we need to deal with internal office politics almost every day. It can be very disappointing to find out that the real customer concern is office politics and this is a concern that may take some time to provide a solution to.

The best way to solve this type of concern is to do your research right from the very start. You need to know who the decision makers are in the company. There will also be people who can influence the decision and you also need to know who they are.

You'll need to try to create rapport with all of the key decision makers and influencers in the company. This will most likely take some time and you'll probably need to make quite a number of sales calls before you can accomplish this.

If you're successful at creating a relationship with all of the key decision makers and influencers, there is a chance that this relationship will be able to overshadow any office politics that may be going on inside the organization.

It is crucial that you don't get yourself involved in internal politics. Once you're able to develop a relationship with the key decision makers and influencers you will likely be exposed to talks about what is going on in the organization. Its fine to listen but it would be better if you kept your opinions to yourself.

Lack of Funds

Lack of funds is a concern that you'll be encountering from time to time. If you're selling to a company and there has already been a purchase request created, there is a good chance that the company has already set aside a budget for the offering.

Now, all you need to do is to provide easier payment terms and this is a matter that you'll need to discuss with your company. Find out what are the best payment terms that you can provide. Sometimes a company will be willing to provide payment terms which are not advertised and these can be provided depending on the assumed revenue of the account.

If you're selling to an individual, you might not have that much room in providing easier payment terms. This is why it is important that you do not offer the best terms in your initial presentation. Give yourself enough room to negotiate. Your negotiation skills will play a big part in providing solutions to this type of concern, but know that you have almost completed the deal.

When a customer has this type of concern, the interest in buying your product has already been established. You won't need to do anymore selling as you will only need to find a solution to the customer's financial problem.

Conclusion

Customers simply won't buy if they do not see the value in your offering. It is your job as a sales person to create this value. This is precisely why planning and preparation play a big part in selling.

Before you head for a sales presentation, ask yourself what customer values will you need to focus on. Will this particular customer be concerned with the financial, functional, or emotional value of your product? In what direction should you be leading the conversation to?

"Sales" is like a game of chess. In order to win a game you need to have a plan. You also need to find out what your opponent's plan is.

Every move you make needs to draw certain responses from the customer. List down all of the possible responses that you can think of and how you can make the customer come to a conclusion in your favor.

Always make sure that you are three steps ahead of your opponent. If you have enough foresight to plan the whole game, do so.

Knowing what questions to ask and how the customer will respond is the key to creating value. Your product has value but it is up to you how you can make the customer realize its value to them.

Keep in mind that before you can sell a product you need to sell a belief. That belief is value. Imagine yourself as a Christian missionary selling Christianity in a country with totally different religious views.

Why would people with a different religion believe in Christianity? How can you make them change their fundamental religious beliefs?

Customers won't buy if you can't make them believe in the value of your product. Sell the value first before you sell the product.

Chapter 12

The Art of Handling Customer Objections

If a customer objects he is giving you an opportunity to sell

Otherwise he'll just show you the door

Chapter 12

The Art of Handling Customer Objections

An objection is an opportunity, never think about it as anything else. In sales, opportunities come in many different forms. Sometimes they come in a form of a problem. If the customer gives you a problem he is asking you to provide a solution. If you can provide an acceptable solution you can close the deal. If you can't provide a solution, the customer will buy from someone else.

A customer will buy; there is no doubt about that. It's just a question of whether the customer will buy from you or from another sales person.

In sales, handling customer objections is a skill that every sales person needs to develop. Without such a skill, a sales person is reduced to being only an order taker. If there are no objections than there is only the matter of taking the order or the customer leaving without buying anything.

It is important to remember that the only reason why a customer objects is because that customer has not found the reason to buy the product.

Customer objections can be classified into two categories:

- I don't see why
- I don't see how

If you look closely, you'll find that these two categories fall under one category and that is the customer does not understand. The customer does not understand and that is why the customer won't buy from you. It is your job as a sales person to make the customer understand.

Let's take a closer look at the "I don't see why" category.

The objections under this category are;

- There is no need

    The first objection under this category is that the customer is not interested in your product. The customer does not have a reason to be interested. When a customer says that he or she is not interested, it is important to take note of when this was mentioned. Was the customer not interested right from the very start or were you able to begin your presentation before the customer lost interest?

If the customer is not interested right from the very start than this can either mean that you didn't do your market research or the customer does not have enough time to listen.

If you didn't do your market research then you're most likely barking up the wrong tree. Every product has a market and you simply can't sell a product to the wrong market. Find out what your market is and focus on that market. Don't waste your time trying to sell to a market that obviously has no need for your product.

Now, if the customer does not have any time to listen to your presentation, you either made the wrong approach or the customer just simply does not have the time and the presentation needs to be scheduled for another date.

The first few minutes of a sales call is critical. It's like creating a web page. People do not read everything in a web page immediately. They first scan the page and see if they are interested. If they are not interested in the fist scan, they move on to another website.

In the first few minutes of your sales call you need to be able to capture the customer's attention. You need to be able to provide value or the customer simply won't listen to you anymore. Keep in mind that customers are always busy. If they give you an appointment that means that there is a small amount of interest in your product. Make sure that your approach will give value to the customer immediately so that you can go on with your presentation.

- There is no urgency

    You need to keep in mind that all of your customers will already have a plan. They plan their day, their events, their work, their business, everything has a plan. Your job as a sales person is to ensure that your product fits within the customer's plan and preferably will have a priority.

    Why is it important that your product has a priority? The longer you wait for a customer to make a decision, the higher the chances are of another sales person offering their products.

    It is your job as a sales person to create urgency.

- You're not the right sales person or the right company

    There are many ways that a customer can say that you are not the right person or you don't represent the right company for them to make a purchase. Some of these ways may not seem so obvious, so you need to listen attentively.

    The reason why the customer thinks that you are not the right person or you don't represent the right company is mainly because you weren't able to create a relationship. Keep in mind that creating rapport is essential to a sales process. If you fail to create rapport then you will likely encounter this type of objection.

- The customer already has a supplier

    Some customers are loyal to their suppliers. This can be because their current supplier provides excellent services or prices, or it will be inconvenient to move to another supplier.

    If you encounter this type of objection then you have failed to make the customer understand the value of your product or services. Loyalty can only be shifted if there is a huge reason to make the shift. If you can provide that reason, then the customer will do everything necessary to shift to you, even if it will cause some inconvenience.

Now, the following objects fall under the "I don't see how" category:

- Your product will not work for the customer

    When a customer gives you this type of objection, you need to find out why. You need to know the reason why because a) the customer may have misunderstood your presentation or b) you've been barking up the wrong tree all along.

    Again, make sure that you research your market thoroughly.

- The customer does not have the funds

    If a customer does not have the funds then you have failed to provide value. Keep in mind that if there is value, then the customer will find the means to purchase your product. There is no such thing as "no funds". However, there is such a thing as "no value" and this is what you need to provide.

- Higher authority will not approve of the purchase

    Again, the customer did not see the value of your product. Now, if you receive this type of objection this can only mean that you are presenting to an influencer and not the decision maker. Keep in mind that there is no difference between making a sales presentation to an influencer and making a sales presentation for a decision maker.

    If the influencer is not convinced of the value of your product, then this can only mean that he or she does not know how to convince the decision maker.

Chapter 13

Tying it all Together

If you were considering a career in sales and didn't know where to start then hopefully this book can become a stepping stone. Every sales person needs to have and apply a sales process. Without one, you'll likely be living a hit and miss career.

Your career in sales will rely on the system you use to approach customers and close deals. If you don't have a system from day one, you'll be lucky to even get to the point where you can develop a system of your own.

If you happen to gat a sales position with a monthly salary, a company will quickly terminate your services if you don't perform. If you get a sales position that only pays commissions on every sale, make sure you have enough funds to support yourself until the day your sales start coming in.

Sales is a challenging but rewarding career. If you perform well, you'll be able to achieve your dreams in no time. If you don't perform, then you had better start looking for another career because you won't last in this one.

The S.A.L.E.S = $OLD method will put you on the right track from the very first day you start your career in sales. If you've been in sales for quite some time but have not managed to improve your career, then this method will help you improve your performance.

The secret to a successful career in sales is simple. You need to understand why and how customers buy and your sales process should meet their buying process. Sales is all about providing solutions to your customers. Every customer has a reason why they will buy. The sales person who can provide the solution will win the deal.

Choose your product carefully

While there may be some truth to the saying that the best sales people can sell anything, this is something that the best sales people simply don't do. The best sales people learn how to choose their products carefully and this is one of the reasons why they are successful.

Is the product that you are selling something that you are interested in? Do you have faith in your product?

You can't sell something that you don't like. You can't convince another person to buy something that you wouldn't buy for yourself if you had the chance.

Sales is not like medicine where there are general practitioners and there are specialists. In sales, there are only specialists. You need to specialize in your product in order to have a fruitful career.

Some sales people are great in selling real estate, but they won't necessarily be good at selling insurance policies. This can be because they are more interested in real estate than they are in insurance policies.

If you are still thinking about a career in sales, make sure that you choose your product wisely. Embarking on a career selling a product that you have no interest in will just be a waste of time and energy. Choose a product that you are passionate in and you will have less difficulty in selling that product.

It won't matter what type of sales process you apply if you are not interested in the product you are selling. However, if you are passionate about your product, then your sales process will work miracles for you.

Learn how to Cope with Rejections

Sales is a tough job. In fact, it's so tough that you'll be spending more time handling rejections than you will closing deals, unless of course you're selling a highly specialized product that no other company produces.

Rejections are part of the every day lives of sales persons. There will be days when all you will get are rejections but don't let these take away your spirit to succeed. Even the best sales people have their fair share of rejections. No one has a 100% batting average. Not everybody you approach will be interested in your product.

However, the more you hone your selling skills, the fewer rejections you'll be facing. Why? This is simply because you will learn how to choose your prospects wisely. You will learn which type of prospects you can spend your time on and which ones you simply need to let go so that you can move to another prospect.

The best way to handle rejections is to be polite. A particular customer may not buy from you now, but there is still a possibility that the customer will buy from you in the future. If you can create a good impression with the customer, chances are you'll be the person that customer will be looking for in the future if and when he or she requires your product.

Provide After Sales Support

One of the worst habits of sales people is not providing after sales support. After they've closed the deal, they let other departments within their company handle anything else that their customers may need. If the customer has further questions on the product, the customer needs to call technical support. If there are billing concerns, the customer calls the billing department.

As a sales person, your job is not completed once the customer hands over a check or signs a contract.

Your customer needs to be totally satisfied with the product or service that they are receiving and it is your job to ensure this.

Why would you need to provide after sales support? Keep in mind that customers will be more inclined to purchase products from people or companies that they trust. If your customer buys from you then there is a good chance that your customer also trusts you.

A customer's trust is everything for a sales person. Trust is the reason why customers become loyal to a brand or a company. Trust is also the reason why companies grow and become stable. Many companies focus their marketing campaigns on creating a trustworthy image and as a salesperson you need to be doing the exact same thing.

For sales professionals, the best way to develop a customer's trust is to provide support even after the sale has been closed. The sales person needs to make sure that the product was delivered in accordance to the terms of the sale and that the customer is fully satisfied.

Should the customer have any concerns with the product, the salesperson should be the first to know so that the concern can be routed to the proper department and acted upon immediately.

Providing after sales support is your key to creating a lasting relationship with your customers. If you can develop this relationship, you are practically assured of a long and fruitful career in sales no matter what product you sell or what company you represent.

www.ingramcontent.com/pod-product-compliance
Lightning Source LLC
Chambersburg PA
CBHW060856170526
45158CB00001B/385